Kylie Fox is a writer, editor, transcriptionist and mother-of-five. Her short crime fiction stories have won awards, including the Dorothy Porter Award, part of Sisters in Crime's annual Scarlett Stiletto Awards, and are published in anthologies. Kylie is currently undertaking a degree in criminal justice and looks forward to studying further in the field of criminal psychology. *Invisible Women* is Kylie's first true crime book.

Ruth Wykes has worked in a range of jobs that have brought her in contact with people in vulnerable social circumstances, including prisons, and maintains an active interest in justice and human rights. Ruth's previous book, *Women Who Kill*, was published by The Five Mile Press in 2011.

INVISIBLE WOMEN

POWERFUL AND DISTURBING STORIES OF MURDERED SEX WORKERS

KYLIE FOX AND RUTH WYKES

echo

echo

Echo Publishing
A division of The Five Mile Press
12 Northumberland Street, South Melbourne
Victoria 3205 Australia
www.echopublishing.com.au

Part of the Bonnier Publishing Group
www.bonnierpublishing.com

First published 2016

Edited by Kyla Petrilli
Cover design by Luke Causby, Blue Cork
Front cover photograph © Joseph Dennis
Page design and typesetting by Shaun Jury

Typeset in Janson Text, Trixie and Univers Condensed

Printed in Australia at Griffin Press.
Only wood grown from sustainable regrowth forests is used in
the manufacture of paper found in this book.

National Library of Australia Cataloguing-in-Publication entry
    Creator: Wykes, Ruth, author.
    Title: Invisible women : powerful and disturbing stories of
    murdered sex workers / Ruth Wykes and Kylie Fox.
    ISBN: 9781760067434 (paperback)
    ISBN: 9781760067465 (ebook : epub)
    ISBN: 9781760067472 (ebook : mobi)
    Subjects: Murder victims–Australia.
    Prostitutes–Australia–Social conditions.
    Prostitution–Social aspects–Australia.
    Other Creators/Contributors: Fox, Kylie, author.
    Dewey Number: 364.15230994

Twitter/Instagram: @echo_publishing
Facebook: facebook.com/echopublishingAU

*For the forgotten, fallen women whose
lives mattered more than they knew.*

CONTENTS

INTRODUCTION

One woman dies while walking home at night and her murder sparks a national outpouring of grief, and a manhunt on a scale that is rarely seen in this country. Another woman is murdered at work, by a client, and barely a ripple is raised. Why is one murder deemed a national tragedy, and the other doesn't seem to matter at all?

It's a familiar story. A small article appears in the paper about a murder and it piques our interest for a moment. As we read on, and the circumstances reveal themselves, we realise it was just a sex worker and we look away. *Serves her right for putting herself in danger*, we think. *She asked for it. We don't care.*

What if that same story was about your sister or your best friend and her job wasn't mentioned? What if the media told you that a young mother went to work in an office, and that afternoon her boss told her to go outside and wash his car. She said no. He got angry and punched her in the face. These might seem like absurd comparisons. But are they? A woman who engages in sex work is just doing her job. If she consents to give a particular service to a client, it doesn't give them the right to brutalise her or take her life.

When we began to research this book, the lack of information about murdered sex workers almost overwhelmed us. It seems that the more labels that are attached to a woman, the less human she becomes to other people. So a street-based, drug-addicted, homeless sex worker could disappear and it appears that nobody pays much attention.

The premise of this book is not to paint sex work in any light other than what it is. It is work. It is the transaction of some form of sexual service in exchange for money. But the women we have written about are among the most vulnerable in society. Most of the cases involve street-based sex workers. On a daily or weekly basis they go to work in a job that doesn't afford them the same protection the rest of us take for granted. There are few rules, no job description, no sick leave, no holiday pay, no minimum wage … and very little protection.

***

Sex work has been present in Australia at least since European settlement. Whether it's brothels, escorts or so-called red light districts, these services have existed for two basic reasons: they offer clients a vehicle for safe, relatively anonymous sex, and also sometimes a way to experience things their partners are unwilling to engage in.

Women who work in the sex industry do so for one basic reason: to earn money. It is important to acknowledge that for many Australian women in the commercial sex industry it is a conscious choice they are happy to make, and they work in the business to help them achieve other life goals – to put themselves through university, to pay off a mortgage more quickly, or because the money is great and the friends they make give them a real sense of community.

For some Australian women it is much more complex. The

road to St Kilda (Melbourne), and to other streets throughout the country that have become the workplaces of street-based sex workers, isn't straight. Neither is it a road many women know they are travelling until they arrive there.

This is a road for women who may have fallen through the cracks of our society. Women who, as children, found themselves in the confusing world of foster care; a world where, far too often, paedophiles are circling, ready to groom, persuade and abuse those least equipped to tell, or to fight back.

Women who don't remember the first time they were sexually assaulted. They were too young. And it happened so often, accompanied by words of love – or threats of punishment and pain. Those women know sex means nothing now; it's a tool, a weapon, a way to get what they need to survive.

Other women who were so young when they fell in love. They made excuses the first time their partner hit them, when he controlled their money, when he isolated them from their friends, from their family.

Women who, as children, lost a parent, a sibling, a friend and who stayed too quiet, bottling up their sadness until one day they were introduced to a drug that – for the first time in their young lives – took their pain away. Rebellious teenagers who, in an act of youthful defiance, said yes to a friend who offered them speed … it felt incredible.

Women with no money, no networks of family or friends, very poor job prospects – for whom the taste of an opiate would take away their pain, or the buzz of amphetamine would make them feel amazing for a while.

Sometimes it is about mental illness and the scarcity of support. The need for survival may lead women to this place. Mental health services in Australia are under-resourced, and completely inadequate to meet the needs of our burgeoning population. The trend towards de-stigmatising mental health has led to an enormous increase in homelessness. They are among the most vulnerable people in Australian society – and the most ignored.

It is these women: the homeless, mentally ill, abused, assaulted, drug-dependent members of society who are most at risk of having to become street-based sex workers. They are the women society has discarded, de-funded, disowned. It beggars belief that when they are injured or killed, people proclaim that it is their own fault, that they put themselves at risk.

When people think about street-based sex workers, they have preconceived ideas. Media reporting and pop culture haven't helped because they reinforce the stereotype of a desperate junkie, someone who hasn't found a way to fit in with our society, who leads a high-risk lifestyle. Someone they simply don't understand.

In reality no little girl, while she is growing up and finding her way in the world, harbours a dream to stand on a street corner in the middle of a freezing cold night and exchange sex with strangers for money. No little girl imagines that sex will be the one skill she will have to exchange for her survival as an adult.

The average age of starting out as a street-based sex worker is 13 – barely even a teenager. Thirteen. It doesn't matter whether people want to keep their heads in the sand or not; the truth is that there are paedophiles in Australia, they're organised and they're active. When children who have endured their abuse grow too old for them, they are discarded. Already damaged, distrustful of authority, believing there is no place in society where they fit, they look for ways to survive. They often find those ways on the streets among people who will accept them, support them and not judge them.

***

In Australia, the majority of sex workers choose to work as escorts or in brothels, rather than as street workers. However, there are pockets in every major city that are known places for kerb crawlers to go in search of quick, anonymous sex. Currently it is estimated that between 1 and 2 per cent of sex workers are street-based.[1] This is in contrast to the rest of the world where more than 80 per cent of sexual services are transacted from the streets.

Of course the risks are greater. The very nature of the work requires these women to get into cars with strangers, or to go into dark alleys and engage in some form of sex. Once they are alone with a customer they are at his mercy, and it is not uncommon for the customer to take more than he has paid for. Although it is difficult to find accurate figures, some studies have shown that 80 per cent of street-based sex workers have experienced some form of violence in the last six months of working.[2] This violence can take many forms: refusal to use a condom, slapping, beating, assaulting, raping, abducting, stealing money and refusing to pay. Sometimes the violence leaves a woman so badly injured she is unable to work for days or weeks. Women are abducted for days at a time and held as sex slaves before being released.

Crimes against sex workers are rarely reported. A major reason for this is the legal status of their job. Depending on what kind of sex work they engage in, or where they operate from, they are often working outside the law. The law varies in the different states of Australia, but street-based sex work is not legal anywhere. When sex workers are raped or beaten they are often too afraid of the consequences of reporting the crime, and of being on the radar of the local police, to do anything about it. Another reason for the reluctance to report is that workers do not believe police will take them seriously. There are numerous historical cases where police have treated sex workers as more criminal than victim.

Street-based sex workers accept these increased risks, or simply feel there is no alternative. It would be simplistic to think we can understand the reasons, but for those who are out there it is preferable to working in brothels because the hours are more flexible, the pay is better and they get to be their own boss.

Another factor is that the majority of street-based sex workers are addicted to illicit drugs. Sex work is a quick, easy way to make the money they need to feed their addictions. It's a moot point: did they turn to the streets because they needed to fund a heroin addiction, or were they on the streets for other reasons, and began to take heroin as a coping tool? There is no clear cut answer, but it is generally accepted that almost all street-based sex workers are addicted to drugs. Addiction is a terrible disease that is given neither the respect nor the compassion by law makers and enforcers that it needs.

***

It's not possible to ignore the feeling, the sense, that among the faceless men are the lonely, the ones who are scanning for a quick exchange of sex for cash, the curious, the judgemental, the overstimulated clans of teenagers. And the predators. There are men who are opportunistic; men who see themselves as ordinary, yet when they are with a sex worker, somehow they see themselves as entitled. She is offering a service for payment, but he decides he's paid for her and can use her in any way he sees fit. The other type of predator, thankfully more rare, is habitual, sadistic, and totally without remorse.

You can't tell by looking if a man is a hunter. More often than not he masquerades as normal; he makes sure you can't see him because he has planned the hunt, prepared for it. He has fantasised about it for so long that it is truth in his head, long before it turns into behaviour.

It may surprise people to know that a predator doesn't pick up sex workers because they're prostitutes. While it's true they are more likely to be a target for violence than other women, it's not because they're sex workers ... it's because they're there.[3] They are accessible, and they are perceived to be less likely to have someone to go home to at the end of the day – they may not be missed as quickly as a woman who might be abducted in a shopping centre car park.

To the collective conscience it began with Jack the Ripper in London. To this day the images remain strong: a mystery man materialised from the fog in Whitechapel, restrained and sadistically murdered a woman, then simply vanished ... until the next time. Even though these murders took place almost 130 years ago, people remain fascinated with 'Jack'. Can those same people recall the name of even one of his victims?

Street-based sex workers remain an obvious target for some predators. American serial killer Gary Ridgeway was the Green River Killer who, during the 1980s and 1990s, murdered at least 49 women and girls in Washington State. Most of his victims were sex workers or women in vulnerable situations, including underage runaways. When DNA caught up with him he confessed to double that number. When asked why he chose sex workers as his victims, his answer was illuminating: 'I picked prostitutes as victims because they were easy to pick up without being noticed. I knew they would not be reported missing right away and might never be reported missing. I picked prostitutes because I thought I could kill as many of them as I wanted without getting caught.'[4]

Australia has its share of predators who have targeted sex workers. Men like Donald Morey who is languishing in a Western Australian prison. He was convicted in 2005 for the attempted murder of a sex worker in Perth, and is the prime suspect in the murder of another sex worker and in the disappearance of a woman who had no connection to the sex industry. Bandali Debs, better known to the Australian public for murdering two police officers in 1998, also killed two young sex workers a couple of years before. Gregory Brazel is often described as one of Australia's most violent prisoners. He is perhaps best known for stabbing Chopper Read, but Brazel murdered two sex workers in 1990 and the female owner of a hardware store earlier in 1982. Former paramedic, Francis Fahey, wore his ambulance-issue boots when he murdered two sex workers in Queensland in 2002 and 2003.

As previously discussed, violent crime against sex workers is not uncommon. Many of the perpetrators may see women as less than human – particularly if they are women who sell sex to survive. Sometimes these crimes against women are impetuous, and with the increasing scourge of methamphetamines in society, behaviours are becoming even more aggressive and less predictable. However, there are many times where the assault is fantasised about, thoroughly planned, and then acted out. There might not be a better example of this than Adrian Ernest Bayley, the man who became the target of a manhunt when he raped and murdered Jill Meagher in 2012, while on parole for previous violent assaults against women.

It is impossible to know the extent of Bayley's crimes in the early 2000s when he trawled St Kilda in search of victims. It is a matter of public record that when he was caught at that time, he was charged with having raped and brutalised five sex workers, yet there were at least 10 other women who were assaulted, held against their will and raped by Bayley, but who refused to press charges or even report him to the police.

Adrian Bayley had perfected a trap that made it impossible

for his victim to escape until he had taken everything he wanted. He would pick up his victim, after negotiating a service with her, and then drive into a nearby laneway in Elwood. He would park his car so close to a wall that it was impossible for the woman to open the door and escape.

Court judge Anthony Duckett was horrified by Bayley's crimes and told him, 'Your response to pleading, cries of pain and tears was to force these women into further sex acts.'[5] Despite his revulsion at Bayley's behaviour, the judge handed down a relatively light sentence. Bayley served only eight years in prison. Even Tom Meagher, the husband of Bayley's murder victim, Jill, later said that Bayley had exposed an inequity in how the justice system treated those attacks.

Bayley only came to the national consciousness when he attacked a different kind of woman. Jill Meagher was just as accessible to Bayley as any of the sex workers from his earlier attacks. Jill could have been anyone but she just happened to be there. The difference this time, the reason the sex workers were horrifically attacked but survived and Jill was murdered, was that this time Bayley knew he had picked the 'wrong kind' of victim. Jill would report her attack. Jill would believe police would track her rapist down. Bayley wasn't going to stand for that. He was determined to remain free so he could continue his predatory and sadistic attacks on women.

***

Violent crimes against sex workers are less frequently experienced in legal brothels, although they still happen from time to time. Brothels have rules, accountability, people on the premises and varying levels of security. This begs the question: if street work is so much more dangerous than working in a brothel, why don't the women get safer jobs? The answer is multilayered, but the easiest way to understand it is to realise that brothels keep up to 60 per cent of the takings, and they have rules that some street-based workers would find impossible to adhere to. Rules such as no drugs while working, no drug addicts, working to a roster, monthly health checks, but mostly a lot less money for doing the same thing they do on the street.

The question also presumes that all sex workers are equal, and have the same needs and aspirations as each other. It assumes that brothel owners/managers don't share the mainstream community's contempt or pity for their street-based sisters. The reality is that brothels have a fairly low opinion of street-based workers and will not employ them. Words like 'dirty junkies', 'unreliable', 'thieves' all came from the mouth of one madam who didn't hold back when explaining her disinterest in employing street-based workers.

There is a hierarchy in the sex industry. At the top are the high-class escorts who command hundreds of dollars an hour. And the bottom? Those people who have the least resources, who are most at risk, or as one hysterical journalist described them when writing about murdered street-based sex workers from Queensland's Fortitude Valley, 'the bottom feeders of the Queensland sex industry'.[6]

***

The Asian sex trade is an issue that nobody wants to talk about. Or if they do, they whisper about sex slaves, human trafficking, underworld crime or women who come to Australia to undercut the locals: better prices, more options, higher-risk sex.

It's difficult to separate the truth from the various myths that exist. Many Asian women work out of illegal brothels and escort agencies, language barriers are real and cultural differences play a part.

Does human trafficking happen in Australia? Absolutely. There are documented cases of women from countries such as China, Thailand and Malaysia being recruited. Typically they and their families are in poverty and would be lucky to earn the equivalent of $100 a month back home. The promises sound enticing. Go to Australia and go to school, or work in a karaoke bar. You'll make lots of money; you'll be able to support your family. We will pay your airfare and accommodation and you can pay us back out of your wages. There'll be plenty of money left for you to send your family, and to be able to spend yourself.

It's enticing. Of course the reality for some women is very different. Once they're through Australian immigration with their sponsor they are whisked off to a small, cramped, overcrowded apartment where the truth of their situation is explained to them. Coercion, violence and drugs are often used to enforce their new reality. They will service men, and they will like it – or they won't get paid. Rarely do these women ever pay off their loans. Creative bookkeeping ensures that they will continue to owe their sponsor money, long after they have repaid their 'debt'.

There are many other Asian women who come to Australia with their new western husband. It all goes well until it doesn't, and when the marriage ends, a number of women find themselves adrift in a strange land. They are often unskilled, have poor English, and work is hard to come by. They often end up engaged in sex work for survival.

Many other women make conscious choices to come to Australia to engage in sex work. Immigration law makes it almost impossible for single Asian women to come to Australia, so they find sponsors in their home country. They come here to make money, to be able to support their families back home.

For every legal brothel in Melbourne there are four illegal ones. Often working from shopfronts that offer therapeutic massage, or from temporary dwellings that are easy to shut down, they have sprung up all over Australia. And they appeal to their customers. They offer services at cheaper rates than the legal brothels and escort services, and are sometimes willing to engage in riskier behaviours.

Because illegal brothels operate outside the law, they are not compelled to honour any of the safe work practices that are rigorously applied to their legal counterparts. Distress buttons, security, regular health checks and the mandatory use of condoms may or may not be adopted.

Very few people know the real names of the workers, or anything about them, so how would anyone know if they go missing? The truth is that unless someone discovers a body, nobody does know. When Chinese escort Ting Fang was murdered in Adelaide on New Year's Day 2015, it took days to formally identify her and notify her relatives in China. When the badly decomposing bodies of 'Jenny' and 'Susan' were discovered in a bedroom in a Sydney apartment in 2008, nobody knew them or anything about their murders. This was despite the fact that the women had died horrifically in an apartment they shared with 11 other people. In 2000, a woman known as 'Bambi' was shot in an illegal brothel in Queensland and her 12-year-old daughter was abducted and raped. Yet nobody seemed to know anything about it.

***

The Australian justice system has come under well-deserved fire in recent years for weighing up the relative value of victims, and imposing lighter sentences when the victim has been perceived to be 'high risk'. The murder of Grace Ilardi highlighted this. Grace was 39 years old when she was murdered in Elwood in 2004. Her killer fled not only the scene but the country. He eventually came back to face justice. Quincy Detenamo was an Olympic weightlifter from the small Pacific nation of Nauru. He said he was sorry, he didn't mean to kill her … things just got out of hand. Newspapers denounced Grace as 'just a prostitute' and described Detenamo as a 'fallen hero'. The weight given to one life over another was too great. He was acquitted of murder and found guilty of manslaughter. Detenamo was sentenced to serve less than 10 years in prison.

Police have often been guilty of not treating crimes against sex workers as seriously as they should. Perhaps an insight into their attitudes is a cartoon that used to hang on a wall in an interview room in one Australian police station. It depicted a sex worker who was up before a judge who said, 'How do you know it was rape?' to which she replied, 'Because the cheque bounced.'

The sign has been removed, along with some of the preconceived ideas that police have had about sex workers. Although attitudes among police have shifted in the last decade, women are still reluctant to report. They are also wary of having a profile with police as they are fully aware that both their sex work and drug use are viewed as criminal behaviour.

***

When the bodies of two women were found floating in the Adelaide River, a muddy crocodile-infested river just south of Darwin, Northern Territory police braced themselves for the media onslaught.

This was going to be a pressure cooker. It had all the ingredients of a case that would bring the national media spotlight to the Territory: sex, drugs, bodies thrown to the crocs, a double murder, teenage suspects and interstate pursuit. And this was one part of Australia where the police force understood how intensely the press would scrutinise their every move. Experience had taught them this years ago when a couple claimed that a dingo had taken their baby from their campsite at Uluru.

Nothing happened. Once it became apparent that the victims were *only* prostitutes – and foreign ones at that – the media seemed to make a collective judgement that this wasn't a story worthy of the nation's attention. Besides, both the media and the public remained preoccupied with another Territory case that had happened almost three years previously – the disappearance of British backpacker Peter Falconio, somewhere in the outback.

Why did the media feed the Australian public an almost daily diet of the mysterious disappearance of a young tourist and pursue his girlfriend, Joanne Lees, halfway around the world yet practically ignore the murder of two women and the callous way their bodies were disposed of?

It is a question which, in one form or another, raised its ugly head numerous times during the research for this book. It became such a predictable, recurring theme – lack of media interest, lack of public information. To the media, the murder of most of these women seemed worthy of little more than a salacious headline: 'Sports Star Kills Prostitute', 'Sex Worker Dies in Hotel'.

Why is it that the public care about the death of some women and not others? In Perth between 1996 and 1997 there was a cluster of disappearances and murders thought to have been committed by the Claremont Serial Killer. Three young women disappeared, and two of them were later found murdered. The prevailing view amongst women all over Perth at the time was, 'It could have been me.' Women responded with gut-clenching fear, and changed their own behaviour – and sometimes their appearance – to avoid drawing the attention of a monster. It was the most talked about crime in Perth for decades. The victims were middle-class and respectable and they all disappeared while enjoying a night out with friends. The city was horrified, terrified – and the public pressure to track down the Claremont Serial Killer was unprecedented. While the cases remain unsolved, they are still talked about with emotion and anxiety in Western Australia.

In 1998, Lisa Brown disappeared from the streets of Perth. In 1999, Jennifer Wilby vanished. Then in 2003, Darylyn Ugle was murdered. All three women were sex workers. When Lisa disappeared, some people worried that the Claremont Killer had changed his modus operandi, because Jennifer Wilby died soon after. Police rushed to reassure the public that this was different, and there was nothing to be alarmed about. Then Darylyn Ugle was murdered, but police and media reinforced their message to the public: there was no link. Many people took the view that Lisa was a drug-addicted prostitute who put herself at risk. Sympathy for her plight and the deaths of Jennifer and Darylyn was difficult to find.

This kind of victim-blaming is misleading and naive.

In September 2012, a beautiful young woman disappeared from Brunswick: Jill Meagher. For a week, Melburnians were fixated on the story. When an arrest was made and her body subsequently discovered, the details of the crime horrified people. The depth of public feeling could be measured in the march to honour Jill Meagher that attracted more than 30 000 people.

In July 2013, the papers ran a story that a sex worker had been murdered in her van in St Kilda. Her name was Tracy Connelly but it took the media almost a week to reveal that. Tracy was part of the St Kilda landscape; she had been on the scene for a long time and was loved by many people. She was addicted to heroin, and so was her partner, Tony. He would sit and spot for her, carefully copying down registration numbers of vehicles Tracy left in. She was a hard worker, and supportive and caring to other sex workers. It was on the one night that she and Tony were separated, while he was in hospital, that Tracy was brutally killed.

Despite the fact that both women lost their lives in circumstances that were horrific, and two sets of families and friends were shattered, the general community embraced Jill as if she were one of their own, yet treated Tracy's murder with collective indifference. Was it because ordinary people could relate to Jill, and the circumstances of her murder suggested it could have happened to any of us? CCTV footage was released to the public in both cases. Police were overwhelmed by information they received about the man seen talking to Jill. No viable suspects resulted from the CCTV images near the scene of Tracy's murder. Was it that people genuinely didn't care, or did they believe that a woman they perceived as leading a high-risk lifestyle had brought something like this upon herself? Jill's killer is in prison, while Tracy's remains free.

***

Invisible Women is by no means a definitive book on the different cases of missing and murdered sex workers in Australia. When we began to research the stories we were astounded. It was always our intention to highlight these crimes against women – the ones nobody seemed to want to talk about. We wanted to contribute to the discussion about why some women's lives seem more valuable, in the eyes of the community, than others; why some murders touch us deeply, and leave us feeling diminished, while others don't even register. When we began to research this book we had no idea how difficult it would be to find people willing to talk, or information about the victims of these crimes. There are paper mountains of information about the perpetrators of the crimes, but almost nothing about the victims.

Is the media to blame? Is it their fault that they only give weight to murder when it has an 'angle' that might affect all of us, or when the victim seems especially innocent or the killer likely to strike again? Or do the media merely reflect back to us the society that we have demanded and shaped for ourselves?

Is it TV or the movies that, for years, have created stereotypes and shaped our thinking and learning? Do we really only have sympathy for a sex worker when she is Julia Roberts in *Pretty Woman*, and to our vast relief she is rescued from that life by her knight in shining armour? Do we really believe the other side of the media portrayal of sex workers as dirty, risky, naughty women?

Is it the justice system that historically gives criminals lighter sentences when they have *only* raped a prostitute? Is it religion that – across all faiths – reinforces that sex workers are moral outcasts to be condemned or cured?

Or is it us? Do our own personal values and attitudes prevent us from seeing that different isn't necessarily wrong? Who taught us to think that sex workers are second-class citizens? And why did we choose to believe them? Religion has long influenced people in their views about sex workers. Governments throughout the history of Australia have legislated against sex work. The justice system has punished it, and society has mocked and derided it. Misogyny plays a strong part in the bias against sex workers. Although our country has come a long way in terms of the status of women in Australian society, there still exist strong double standards about the role of women in this country. If a 'nice girl' is still judged by the number of sexual partners she has had, a sex worker carries the weight of condemnation even more heavily on her shoulders.

It took us a long time, and some robust discussion, to decide on who we would highlight in this book. Every woman's story is worth telling, and our eventual decisions were no reflection on the value of the women we haven't been able to include in *Invisible Women*. It was our hope to bring these women to life in a way that might show readers who they really were beyond the headlines: mothers, sisters, daughters, friends, colleagues. Women who loved animals and children, who did the crossword in the newspaper, played Trivial Pursuit and laughed with unbridled joy.

That task was naive, and in many cases insurmountable. For every woman in Australia who has been murdered, they have left behind a network of family and friends whose lives have been shattered by their loss. Yet these living victims of crime don't have access to the same levels of support as people whose loved ones were more 'innocent' victims.

The system needs to change. The cracks in the road need to be paved over. It isn't the sex work or the drug use that creates the dangerous cracks, but the reasons these women are forced to walk that road in the first place.

Change requires compassionate and visionary government across all states and territories of Australia; change that understands there is a place for sex workers in contemporary society, and that legislation needs to be passed to decriminalise sex work.

It requires an honest appraisal of the reasons why women find themselves standing on the street at 3 a.m. – the poverty, homelessness, addiction, mental health issues, domestic violence and criminality that keep street-based sex workers enslaved to a lifestyle they don't want, but can't find a way out of.

It requires the funding of outreach programs and safe houses to help deal with the complex, and incredibly difficult task of helping to affect change in the lives of street-based sex workers.

And it requires us, as ordinary people, to stop victim-blaming when we read that another sex worker has been harmed or killed. And to not look away.

Alongside the higher-profile cases featured in this book the authors have included a series of shorter pieces about whom little is known – these are the real invisible women of the title.

The stories are presented in chronological order, with one obvious exception. The death of Tracy Connelly, and Wendy Squires' subsequent blog post, was the catalyst behind the writing of this book. It seems only fitting the book starts here.

TRACY CONNELLY
21 July 2013

Tracy Connelly's last actions on earth were typical of the caring and compassionate woman that friends and work colleagues loved. Her partner, Tony Melissovas, the man Tracy had loved and shared her life with for nine years, had a severely infected hand. True to form, he refused to go to hospital, even when it had swollen to almost the size of a football, preferring to stay with Tracy and look after her. Tracy, however, was having none of that. She called an ambulance and when the paramedics arrived, convinced Tony to go with them.

Tracy spent the afternoon with Tony in the hospital, lying on his bed and chatting cheerily to keep his mind off the pain in his hand. That night Tracy had to leave to go to work. Tony had serious misgivings though. Usually while Tracy worked, he would loiter quietly in the background keeping an eye out for her and writing down the number plates of each car she drove away in. In recent years he had accumulated more than 3000 registration numbers.

Like most street-based sex workers, Tracy had her own patch of St Kilda where she worked – a place everyone knew as Tracy's Corner. She kissed Tony goodnight and headed back to the Econovan in Greeves Street. No doubt she would have preferred to snuggle under the doona – it was cold outside – but they needed money. She emerged from the van dressed for work – no longer Tracy, she was in her working persona of 'Kelly' – and walked off into the long night.

***

Tony was restless and anxious at the hospital. He hated not being around to protect Tracy. His concerns were abated a little when he received a text from her at around 10.30 p.m. to let him know she was safe and well.

Melbourne was in the midst of a bitterly cold winter and working the streets was hard slog; one can imagine that a paying customer would be a welcome relief from the cold outside. Perhaps Tracy let her guard down a little.

As the night wore on, Tony's anxiety rose. Hours had passed and he hadn't heard again from Tracy, though she'd promised to check in with him throughout the night.

Sunday morning, 21 July 2013, dawned and Tony still hadn't heard from Tracy. Meanwhile, the people of St Kilda went about their business, strolling down Greeves Street towards busier roads, visiting cafes for breakfast, heading to The Esplanade, Luna Park or the bay. Many walked or drove past the silent Ford Econovan, not giving its presence a second thought. The van, which had been home to Tracy and Tony for several months, was a sight locals were accustomed to, and visitors barely noticed it.

Tracy's close friend was asleep in her own van across the road. Their proximity to each other gave them a sense of safety. They had organised the previous day to bunk in together on the Saturday night after work. But there had not been an 'after work' for Tracy, and in any case, her friend had fallen asleep.

Tony grew increasingly worried throughout the morning and, as the morning became afternoon, he could take Tracy's silence no longer. He discharged himself from the hospital and headed home to find her.

Greeves Street was quiet, save from the usual sounds of cars and people going about their business. Tony and a friend went straight to the van he and Tracy shared, hoping to find her fast asleep and apologetic for having worried him unnecessarily. As he slid open the van door, the silence was shattered. Tracy's battered body lay inside.

In a panic, Tony and his friend pulled Tracy out of the van and laid her on the ground, their instinct to revive her. They couldn't see her properly inside the van – it was dark, there was too much blood. Yet even before they managed to gently lay her on the ground, they knew in their hearts it was too late.

She was dead.

A neighbour saw Tony just moments later: 'We saw him after he discovered the body and he was hysterical, uncontrollably crying. I knew straight away something had happened. His face was just … You could just tell he was broken.'

***

Tracy Connelly came from a loving family. At 15, like a lot of girls that age, Tracy started acting out at home, craving her independence and desperately wanting to try new things and make her own decisions. Her father later reflected, 'I don't think she was totally rebellious, but certain friends had a lot more freedom than she did and then Tracy wanted to be with them of course.'[7]

She fell into the trappings of this newfound rebellious lifestyle, trying drugs, drinking and staying out well past curfew. One night, Tracy stayed out until three in the morning and this made her mother furious. Tracy was grounded – no more going out until she could be trusted to return at a reasonable hour. Unhappy with that, Tracy called Child Welfare who talked to her mother and told her that Tracy was old enough to do as she liked. The response 'not under my roof' pushed Tracy's hand and she was found accommodation two days later.

It was in that accommodation, a 'halfway house for drug addicts who were trying to get off the drugs or whatever' that she met a boy, Matthew who she quickly entered into a relationship with, and who then introduced her to hard drugs.[8]

Both Tracy and Matthew became addicted to heroin and then, to support their habit, began sex work. This was a course that was to shape the rest of Tracy's life.

When Tracy had just turned 18, she went and saw her parents to tell them that she and Matthew were expecting a baby. Their initial reaction was one of shock and horror: 'They can't look after themselves! How are they going to look after a baby?'[9]

But their fears seemed to be misguided. For a while, it seemed the baby was the best thing that could have happened. Tracy gave birth to a healthy baby boy who they named Billy, and the couple seemed to be coping well. They doted on the baby, cleaned themselves up and Matthew went back to studying at university.

Then, for reasons still unclear, the couple separated and Matthew took baby Billy to Tasmania where his mother lived. Perhaps the lure of drugs and her previous lifestyle were too strong for Tracy and she thought her baby would be better off without her.

A friend of Matthew's mother was looking after Billy. News filtered through to Tracy's parents about their grandson's whereabouts at around the same time they learned that Matthew had committed suicide. A battle for custody ensued and Billy was eventually returned to Melbourne to live with Tracy's parents who raised him from then on.

Tracy saw Billy a few times but eventually she returned to her life of drugs and sex work and rarely spoke to her family. When Billy was around 10 years old, Tracy's family left Melbourne and settled into a new life on Queensland's Gold Coast. At around this time Tracy fell pregnant again. When the baby was born she gave him up for adoption. Over the years she drifted in and out of her nomadic lifestyle. And then she met Tony Melissovas.

The couple were happy together, moving in with Tony's mother and entering rehabilitation to get off heroin. Clean, Tracy even obtained employment in a cafe, working with Tony's mother. By all accounts she loved the work, she was happy and the job lasted for several years. Things were looking up.

Then, in 2009, Tony's mother died and the pair started a downward spiral. They both returned to using heroin and before long Tracy was back on the streets of St Kilda, working as Kelly, to pay for the drugs.

In late 2012 or early 2013, the Ford Econovan that Tracy and Tony called home broke down and they had it towed to Greeves Street outside the St Kilda Gatehouse, a refuge for street-based sex workers that Tracy frequented. There she felt safe and had a lot of friends. Everybody – other workers, clientele and the social workers who worked at the Gatehouse – thought highly of Tracy, describing her as friendly and cheerful and always willing to lend a helping hand. Her exotic good looks didn't go unnoticed either. Social worker Lucy Valentino remembered, 'I'd rock up to work and there's the van, and there'd be these big long legs coming out of the van and even though Tracy was technically homeless, she'd come out of that bloody van looking like a model.'

Tracy spoke to her friends about getting out of the life, often while baking cupcakes or having a cup of tea at the Gatehouse.

She truly disliked the life she was leading but couldn't see many alternatives. Nonetheless, she was a loved member of her community and many have noted that she never came across as a 'strung out druggie', a label that too easily stereotypes heroin users.

***

When Tracy kissed her boyfriend goodnight and walked away from his hospital bed, neither of them had any clue that they would never see each other again. Tracy never took clients back to their van, preferring instead to go in the client's car to another location. In fact, Tony always held onto the keys, removing any temptation that his partner could be talked into using it. But Tony was in hospital that Saturday night, and Tracy had the keys to the van. Perhaps, without Tony there to watch out for her, without him diligently taking down the registration numbers of each punter, Tracy felt less threatened in the relative safety of her own home, in easy view of the Gatehouse and of her friend who slept in her own vehicle only 20 metres away. Perhaps the cold of that winter night made her desperate to get indoors for a while. Whatever the reason, Tracy found herself in a van with the man who would take her life.

When Tracy's body was found, battered and with extensive injuries to her head and upper body, her handbag, mobile phone and credit card were missing. Was this a robbery gone wrong? Had somebody, presumably a client, decided to rob the few things Tracy owned? Had she fought back, enraging him so that the crime escalated into this brutal murder? Or was murder the intention all along? Perhaps the missing possessions were simply an act of staging by the perpetrator.

Surprisingly, given the brutal nature of the attack, the media remained silent for more than a day. Then came the headlines: 'Homicide police investigate prostitute's death in St Kilda', 'St Kilda prostitute brutally murdered'. The story was simple, its inference clear: a street-walking, heroin-addicted prostitute was dead. Everyone knew she must have led a high-risk life, and put herself in harm's way. This wasn't a crime that affected everybody, it was restricted. The public at large were safe. No newspaper space was wasted, no air time given on television. Tracy's death didn't matter.

But it did matter. It mattered to Tony Melissovas. It mattered to Tracy's family who had spent a lifetime afraid of that particular knock on the door, that horrifying phone call; a call, when it came, that led to Tracy's mother suffering a heart attack. It mattered to the other girls who worked near Tracy and considered her a friend. It mattered to the workers at St Kilda Gatehouse who looked forward to their regular cuppas and a chat with Tracy. And, fortunately, it mattered to a journalist who happened to see Tracy each day on her way to work.

When news of the death broke, *The Age* journalist Wendy Squires wrote a blog about a woman she passed each day, who she occasionally gave coffee to, who was always quick with a bright smile and a wave. Squires didn't know the identity of the murdered sex worker, what she did know was that her friend hadn't been on her usual corner for days. Squires appealed to the universe for the murdered woman not to be Tracy. She spent days trying to establish the identity of the victim. When her worst fears were confirmed, her blog post was quickly updated and 'Her name was Tracy Connelly and she was my friend', a heartfelt and equally heartbreaking story, went viral across social media platforms.

Just as people were starting to sit up and take notice, Tony Melissovas released a photo of himself and Tracy through social media. It was an image taken a few years ago, of the happy couple snuggling in the snowfields. Almost overnight Tracy Connelly became human in the eyes of the public: her smile was warm, her face was open, hopeful, and her eyes were kind. Suddenly Tracy wasn't just some anonymous drug-addicted street worker; she became a real woman with hopes and dreams and a life.

A week after Tracy's murder, Melbourne radio station Joy FM ran a special tribute to Tracy during their weekly show *The Vixen Hour*. Friends of Tracy were asked to talk about her, and their memories made her real, well beyond the headlines that had struggled to even print her name:

> I knew her as a lovely lady, as a friend; helpful to everybody, always sweet, always came in and gave you a kiss g'day and said, 'Hello darls' to everybody. She will be very, very missed. She was a delightful person, wonderful to have a discussion with. Very well spoken. Very articulate. She was lovely.

> I've known Tracy for over 10 years. She was loved by pretty much everybody in St Kilda. She was incredibly warm, very intelligent, exceptionally beautiful – and exceptionally brown, in winter as well. And she was loved by all.

> Tracy, to me, represents – I suppose she's an image of myself because she's worked ever since I've been here. Like, we used to share the same corner – we're talking nearly 20 years ago and she's been there. She's always been around. So just a huge shock and totally devastating.

> I knew Tracy for four and a half years. We saw each other daily. I really connected with her around parenting 'cause she had

some boys and I've got a boy, and she was always interested in how my 12-year-old was doing and whether he was still being a nightmare. Always had really wise words to say, which was awesome. And also the thing about her is that she had the best posture. When I saw her I would always stand up straight. I will remember that forever. If I want a picture in my mind, it's her standing up really straight, looking fabulous – and being an amazing person that cared more about others than she did about herself.

My experience of Tracy as a friend towards me was Tracy saw me walking back to the Gatehouse late one afternoon. I was severely traumatised by some news from the doctor about myself. Her and her partner pulled over and made damn sure that I got to where I needed to go, which was back to the doctors. She would have stopped to help anybody that needed help; she was a very loving, very caring person, and I will miss her terribly.

She was just the most beautiful person. She would bounce into the Gatehouse, always happy. Never want to give you any of her pain. Never showed her pain. Always interested in what everyone else was doing, and – just lovely. Beautiful, beautiful person. Definitely a light's gone out at the Gatehouse now.

I was lucky and privileged and honoured to know the beautiful Tracy. Not only was she exotic and beautiful to look at, she was warm, friendly, and had one of the best senses of humour. I would often see her when I was down in St Kilda, working. She had her own special corner and we'd often have conversations around her special corner because I knew police would probably charge her with loitering. But she assured me she had a lovely relationship with all the people around that particular corner.

I was a very close friend of Tracy's and she was a very beautiful person. She had a heart of gold and she'd do anything for anybody. I love Tracy, and everyone loves her – and that's the way she'll always be remembered.

I remember Tracy as a bit of a character, but a lovely, lovely girl who has been around for a long, long time. Special little things I remember about her was her lovely manners and beautiful posture. She would trot in here on her high heeled boots, and make us all laugh. And trot in and have a drink of cordial, and go back to work. And she had to work. She worked very, very hard.

She was hard to get to know but once you got under that hard exterior she was the sweetest person that you could ever find … and she made boobs out of nothing, and she inspired me. Now I do the same thing.

Tracy Connelly. She was very personable and very polite but she was also funny. Very dynamic in her way. Used to tell little stories about family and how her dad would renovate, then her mum wouldn't like it, then he'd do it the other way. Very dedicated renovator. And little stories about people and things, incidents that had happened.

Tracy was my friend, she's really special. I know that sounds a bit cliché but Tracy really did stand out for me because she gave of herself so much. She gave me more than I could ever have given to her. She was beautiful, she was deep, she will be deeply missed.

The media at large were forced to take notice and several articles were printed about the life of Tracy Connelly. A candlelight vigil, attended by the St Kilda community, Tracy's family and friends, as well as several well-known celebrities, was held to honour the life of Tracy and to bring emphasis to the often invisible and ignored side of Melbourne's nightlife.

What happened in those early morning hours of 21 July? Had someone been watching, someone who knew her routines, her habits? Someone who knew that for the first time in years her minder was not out on the streets this night?

Was it a crime of opportunity? A client who met Tracy and went back to her van with her for sex then saw a chance to rob her? Or was it someone with a more sadistic bent who stole her purse, phone and credit card to mask their real intentions?

Two separate weapons were used to batter the life out of Tracy. The injuries she sustained to her head and chest were horrific – more than were necessary to disable someone in order to steal then flee the scene, more than was 'necessary' to end her life.

Police released CCTV footage that showed Tracy at the corner of Mitchell and Carlisle Streets, St Kilda, at 11.30 p.m. on Saturday, 20 July 2013. Police said CCTV footage showed Tracy with at least one other person within 20 metres of her van between 1.30 a.m. and 2.30 a.m. on Sunday morning. Other CCTV footage of a man walking along the street wearing a jacket and white shoes was also released by police. It is possible that this man inadvertently witnessed something important to the case and police are very keen to speak to him. Yet more footage showed a dark-coloured late-model ute, the owner of which the police are especially keen to speak to.

A year earlier when police released CCTV footage of another wanted man to the public, they had been swamped with tips; the blue-hoodie-clad man had been caught by the cameras of a bridal boutique in Brunswick, he had been talking to Jill Meagher, she was missing. He was identified to police within hours. Police were optimistic that they would have similar success with this CCTV footage, yet no meaningful leads have come from it.

The predator who took Tracy Connelly's life remains at large. Police believe it was a robbery gone wrong. They collected DNA and, although it doesn't match anyone in known databases, it may one day unlock the mystery.

Tracy's friends still talk about her as if she hasn't quite left the building. They relate stories of her life with great affection and sadness. They laugh when they recall stories of her mischief, like the cupcake-making afternoon at St Kilda Gatehouse where, vanilla essence in hand, Tracy added a few drops to the mix then skulled the rest of the bottle. Or of the time she managed to find that one hidden bottle of champagne. They miss that moment where she would burst into the drop-in centre, with a beaming smile on her face and a 'Hello, darls.'

Those closest to Tracy remember her genuine love for Tony. It's common on the streets to have a 'partner', but often it's a relationship of convenience, of mutual need. Tracy and Tony, they say, had a strong connection: solid, tight and genuine. Real love. Tony, according to people who knew him, was broken and guilt-ridden when Tracy was murdered.

In some ways it is amongst her peers that she has left the most yawning of chasms. In any workplace people need mentors, people who have been in the job for a while, who can teach them the ropes, the shortcuts, the tips to keep them safe. Tracy's reputation on the streets was of a careful woman, who was aware of the risks, and who did as much as she could to minimise them. She was known to be a great support to younger workers. Someone who looked out for you. Someone who cared.

In quiet, reflective moments she would say she hated the life. Hated it. She wanted to find a way out. She would talk to people about Billy, about Tony, about what might have been, and what could still be possible.

Tracy Connelly would be surprised if she knew what had happened since her death. She had been in the game for many years, and knew the public's perceptions about her lifestyle. It was a lifestyle she had grown to despise, that she dreamed of escaping. It left her feeling like she wasn't worth very much.

She couldn't have been more wrong.

SHIRLEY BRIFMAN
4 March 1972

Shirley Margaret Brifman was born in Atherton, Queensland, in 1935. When she was a teenager she ran away from home and found herself in Cairns. She found work as a barmaid, fell in love with the owner of the hotel, and married him at the age of 22; Szama 'Sonny' Brifman was 20 years her senior. Shirley began working as a sex worker while still at the Far North Queensland hotel.

By 1958, she was working in one of Brisbane's oldest brothels under the name 'Marge Chapple'. Shirley was a petite woman with a lively personality. She knew a number of police officers, in part because there was rampant corruption at the time, and a number of police had financial interests in brothels. Other police collected protection money from brothels.

In 1963, Shirley and Sonny moved to Sydney. It's likely she wanted to create some distance from Queensland because that year she was the star witness at a royal commission into police corruption. She told numerous lies when giving evidence, but the things she said were enough to unsettle some powerful people. Until 1968, Shirley worked from the lounge of the Rex Hotel in Kings Cross, then she opened brothels in Potts Point and Elizabeth Bay.

In 1971, Shirley and her husband were charged with offences relating to prostitution. They were accused of grooming their underage daughter, Mary Anne, for sex work. Shirley was livid. She had been paying off corrupt police for years, so when they refused to protect her now she blew the whistle on them.

Shirley went on television to make allegations of police corruption. In recorded interviews she named over 50 police from New South Wales and Queensland, and she linked them to specific crimes or corruption. Some of the names she spilled were senior police – and very powerful men.

Shirley fled back to Queensland and in 1972 was living in a safe house, a rented unit in Bonney Avenue, Clayfield, an inner-northern suburb of Brisbane. On Saturday, 4 March, her daughter Mary Anne went into the guest bedroom at 8.30 a.m. and found her mother's lifeless body. Mary Anne later recalled that the night before, a visitor had come to the house and handed Shirley a vial of drugs. The visitor allegedly ordered her to take the contents of the vial or something would happen to her children.

Her death was ruled a suicide, a barbiturate overdose, although there is strong doubt about this finding. At the request of Queensland police there was no inquest.

In 2015, Mary Anne Brifman requested an inquest into her mother's death. Even though 43 years have elapsed, Mary Anne is certain her mother was murdered, and believes she deserves justice.

MARGARET WARD
13 November 1973

Margaret Grace Ward was an 18-year-old woman who worked in a massage parlour in Chermside, Brisbane. The last time Margaret was seen was after leaving a high-profile solicitor's office where she had sought advice about a summons she had received in relation to her work.

A few years after her disappearance, in a climate where five other people had disappeared under mysterious circumstances, police said they believed Margaret knew too much and had talked too much. They were referring to a series of domino events that had occurred after the March 1973 Whisky Au Go Go nightclub firebomb in Fortitude Valley that had killed 15 people.

Margaret was one of three sex workers or brothel owners who died or disappeared during the 1970s, at a time where Queensland's police service was rife with corruption and standover tactics of criminal enterprises commonplace.

One Pub Crawl Too Many
ELAINE KING
12 July 1974

The Australia of 1970 was a very different world for women than the one we live in today. The sexual liberation movement that was sweeping the developed world was still just a ripple around the margins of Australian society. We still preferred our men at work, women in the kitchen, and sex inside marriage. Society changed significantly throughout the 1970s, but at the dawning of the decade, Australia remained deeply conservative.

A woman who fell through the cracks, who didn't have a husband or extended family to support her, did not have the comfort or financial support that contemporary women enjoy. The only government assistance available to a lone mother in 1970 was the widow's pension.

A single mother had to call on her own resources simply to survive. Child care centres were rare and it was really difficult for a woman to work and raise children alone. In 1970 there were relatively few professions for women. It was tough to be single. And to be a mum.

At that time Kings Cross was sleazy, sinful and full of sex. Or that was the way it seemed. Scantily clad women paraded down Darlinghurst Road, smiling salaciously at wide-eyed suburban boys. Men furtively darted in and out of strip shows, and the nightclubs bulged at the seams. It was loud, exciting, exotic and a little bit naughty. It was the first place people thought of when the issue of sex work came up.

Yet it was illegal to be a sex worker. In 1968, the East Sydney brothels had been closed down and the government, not wanting those former employees to spill out onto the streets, introduced a new law into the Vagrancy Act making it an offence to 'loiter for the purposes of prostitution'. Sex workers on the street became a major focus for police, largely because the government wanted to 'protect' American soldiers on leave from Vietnam, and to curb the increasing drug addiction of street-based sex workers.

The 1970s saw the highest number of arrests of street-based sex workers in New South Wales. It made their life hard; not only were the workers repeatedly arrested, they complained that police were asking for $150 a week in extortion to keep the arrests down.

Elaine 'Beverley' King was one of the sex workers who was arrested multiple times in the early 70s for street soliciting and disorderly conduct. People saw her as street-wise and transient, and they knew she had a drinking problem. When she turned up dead in a rent-by-the-hour room in a Haymarket hotel, her room was littered with clues, with evidence that had been left behind. Her murder should have been solved, but it wasn't.

***

Everyone who knew Elaine King called her Beverley. She was born Elaine Yvonne Thow in 1929 on King Island, a narrow island, only 64 kilometres long, which lies in the Roaring Forties between Tasmania and Victoria in the Bass Strait. It might have been an idyllic childhood: endless beaches, bush walks, a place everyone knew you and looked out for you. However, little Beverley had a secret. Her father was regularly sexually abusing her – and she had no place to run.

But run she did as soon as she turned 17. Beverley moved to Melbourne and tried to find her way in the world. She met a man, and that dalliance was intense, brief and over almost before it began. Then she met a sailor, Bob King. They fell in love and were married. It wasn't long before their daughter, Andrea, was born.

In the early 1950s, Bob went to fight in the Korean War. He was only gone for two years, but in that time Beverley's life seemed to come unstuck. She became depressed, and started to drink alcohol; not just an occasional drink, but enough to forget, to cope, to try and numb her pain.

Soon after Bob returned from the war it became obvious their relationship was over. Beverley took Andrea and made her way north. This was the beginning of years of transient living for the now single mother and her child. Beverley struggled to raise her daughter in a time that preceded the supporting mother's benefit. They owned little in the way of material possessions; Andrea rarely attended school, and often went hungry.

For a while Beverley rented a house in Sydney's west at Toongabbie, where she became a regular at the local pub. Not only was it a convenient place to quiet the demons of her alcohol addiction, but it was a great place to meet men. But like many women for whom the scars of abuse hadn't healed over, Beverley chose the wrong ones time and again.

Nobody knows exactly when she started engaging in sex work. Certainly by the time Andrea was 11 years old Beverley's life was transient again. The decision was made that Andrea would go back to live with her father, who by now had remarried. That meant Beverley was alone and unaccountable to anyone.

Beverley worked the streets of Haymarket and inner Sydney. She moved into an apartment in Oxford Street, Darlinghurst, not far from the city and Kings Cross. Life became a series of blurs, of small decisions she made in order to survive. Sex work was the income that helped her stay alive, alcohol was the salve that stopped her feeling the pain.

She was estranged from her family. To those back home on the island she was their dirty little secret, the black sheep that nobody talked about. Her daughter wanted a relationship with her mother but couldn't handle her drinking and lifestyle. The last time she saw her mother would leave her harbouring guilt for the rest of her life. Beverley turned up on Andrea's doorstep blind drunk. Her daughter told her to leave – and not to come back.

On the evening of Thursday, 11 July 1974, 45-year-old Beverley was drinking at the Capital Hotel in Campbell Street in the CBD. She was seen there at around 7.30 p.m. with a man. Hotel patrons later described him as young – in his 20s or 30s. He was wearing ugg boots and drinking Resch's beer. She was later seen at the same hotel with a man; however, nobody was able to say whether it was the same one with whom she had been drinking earlier in the evening.

Then at 9.45 p.m. that evening, Beverley and an unknown man, calling themselves Mr and Mrs Rivers, booked into the Burlington Hotel in Haymarket – almost a kilometre away.

Were they three separate men that Beverley was seen with that evening? The answer to that question has never been found.

The following morning at around 8 a.m., a housemaid opened the door to Room 96 in the Burlington Hotel to a ghastly scene. A woman who was obviously dead lay on her back on the bed, her bra pulled up to just below her neck. A pillow covered her face and another one had been placed on her chest. The woman was covered in bruises. The housekeeper ran to her manager who immediately called the police.

When police arrived they studied the room. Beverley had a dozen separate bruises on her neck. Her slip and knickers were lying on the floor, and another pair of knickers were near her right hip. Police also found bloodied pantyhose. When they lifted the pillow from her face they noticed that there appeared to be something in her mouth – it was $11 in cash. Was this some kind of bizarre message from her killer? Had there been an argument over payment for her services, and the client shoved the cash in her mouth in a cruel 'shut up and have your money, then' statement? Or was it something else?

As police examined the hotel room they collected evidence, including fibres, hairs, cigarettes, beer cans and a receipt for the room. They quickly learned the dead woman's identity, despite the fact that to the hotel she was Mrs Rivers, and set off to interview people. That was no easy task. The people who had been in the area on the Saturday nights were drunks, transients and troublemakers. Witnesses could describe the beer and the ugg boots, but found it more difficult to identify the person wearing them.

When Beverley's autopsy was conducted it was determined that she had died by strangulation, and that a combination of bare hands and a ligature (the pantyhose) had been used to kill her. There was evidence of vaginal and anal penetration, but no sperm was present.

In the 1970s, DNA had not yet been mapped and forensic testing was relatively unsophisticated. Police were able to establish that Beverley was blood type O and that the blood found on the pantyhose was type A. They had no sperm or fingerprints, but they had the killer's blood.

Time went by with no leads, and no resolution. In 1976, a

coronial inquest was held into Beverley King's murder but was unable to identify a suspect.

***

In many ways it is more difficult for police to solve the murder of a sex worker than most other murders they encounter in the course of their work, especially if the victim was working out on the streets. The victim's life is often transient, which means they're not as accountable to friends and family as others whose movements are better known to loved ones. By the nature of their work, street-based sex workers meet a number of strangers every day, and go off to a discreet location with them. Sometimes there is too much evidence, other times there is not enough. When police need to obtain information, they have to ask the victim's friends, often other sex workers, who don't trust them and are reluctant to talk.

If police use the media, it is often of limited value. The accompanying headline generally includes the word 'prostitute', inviting labels, judgement and implying the victim is somehow less deserving of sympathy. It reinforces that the woman who has become the victim of a violent crime is a social and moral outcast. Not worth caring about.

Did this happen to Beverley King? Did the police do everything they could to solve her murder?

In 2012, the NSW Unsolved Homicide Team reinvestigated her case. They announced to the public that a $100 000 reward was on offer for anyone who had information that would resolve this murder. They released information to the media about the man who was wearing ugg boots and drinking Resch's beer. Then they looked for the evidence that had been collected at the Haymarket hotel in 1974. Forensics had come a long way, and it might just be possible that DNA could be extracted from the blood on those pantyhose, or the cigarette butts that had been collected. DNA testing and other advances in science might finally mean the police could unlock the secrets of the murder of Beverley King.

But the evidence was gone. Missing, carelessly misfiled, lost? Nobody knew.

Beverley King's murder had been sadistic, committed by a sexually violent man who took her life in a manner that was as arrogant as it was personal. There was nobody to bear witness to the terror she felt that night, or the physical pain as she lost her life to a stranger.

The little girl who had run away from her childhood home to escape the sexual violence of a man she should have been able to trust had come full circle.

Her murder remains unsolved.

The 19th Hole
SHIRLEY FINN
23 June 1975

When society madam and brothel owner Shirley Finn was found shot dead in her Dodge Phoenix on a fairway of the Royal Perth Golf Club, the Australian media went into a frenzy. This was the beginning of a case that would span decades, incite numerous armchair detectives to speculate on the causes of her fate, and bring into question the reputations of some of Western Australia's top cops and politicians.

There's nothing that the media like more than murder, scandal, sex and corruption – when all of that and more is rolled into one neat package, their thirst is insatiable. Unfortunately, they forgot that behind that big story was a real woman. And she had been cold-bloodedly murdered.

***

Shirley Shewring was born in 1941, a 'war baby'. Her father, an RAAF pilot, barely saw his little girl who was left to be raised by her mother while he was at war. She wasn't a very strict woman, and Shirley was often left to her own devices.

Shirley grew up in a nice, middle-class neighbourhood near

the Swan River in Mount Pleasant. The eldest of three children, she was a good girl, was always helpful to her mother, had a vivacious fun-loving spirit and wonderful smile and was incredibly intelligent.

In fact, as the years went on Shirley continuously topped all of her classes, receiving the highest possible marks for English and maths. In another day and age, Shirley would probably have been recommended for a program for gifted children but in the 1950s girls weren't expected to think about such things. Shirley was supposed to be thinking more about seeking a good husband than filling her head with book learning and ideas of a career.

Shirley hit her teenage years in the 1950s, and her parents, like so many of their generation, were still recovering from the losses that the war had brought to them. While young people were out drinking milkshakes, and dancing to the new style rock 'n' roll music, their parents tried to piece their lives back together. For Shirley's family, it was also a time when they had a new baby boy to look after, and a new house under construction. They were distracted and didn't notice, until it was too late, that their little Shirley was growing up. And growing up fast.

At 14, Shirley looked older than her years and boys started to notice her – and she was noticing them right back. She started to sneak out of her window at night to go dancing and to see the boys she was becoming well-acquainted with.

One night, her father discovered that she was missing from her bed. He searched for her everywhere that he could think to look but there was no sign of the girl. Finally, not knowing what else to do, he called the police and reported Shirley missing.

The police found Shirley a short time later with a 20-year-old man, who she admitted during police questioning to having sex with. It was also discovered that she'd been sexually active before with another older boy. These men were not held responsible – Shirley was. And so were her parents.

Shirley, her mother and her father had to appear before a magistrate. The parents were accused of neglecting their daughter and allowing this kind of 'dirty' behaviour. They pleaded with the magistrate to give them another chance, promising to be tougher on Shirley and to help her to go to church more often, and to join clubs that would keep her out of trouble, but the magistrate would have none of it. He wanted an example set.

Shirley was taken away from her parents, her home and her baby brothers, and handed over to the nuns at the Home of the Good Shepherd at Leederville. There she was expected to work long days in the laundry, sweating in a steam-filled room, for no pay. Conditions were harsh and Shirley began to deteriorate.

It was noted at the time that Shirley had become 'depressed and felt bad, dirty and contaminated'.[10] She was a changed girl; her vivacious spirit and quick smile had evaporated and she instead wore a distant, haunted look.

After eight long months being locked up with the nuns, Shirley was finally allowed to return home to her family. She was just 15 years old. She returned to school, having left at the top of the class, only to discover that she was irreparably behind the rest of the class. She finished out the year and then left school for good.

Shirley got a job in a dress shop not far from home, in Piccadilly Arcade, and it was there that she met Des Finn, a young man in the RAAF.

The pair hit it off immediately and began vying for every minute they could to spend together. Shirley's parents forbade the relationship, having learnt their lessons last time. But Shirley would have none of it. She knew her own mind – and heart – and was determined to continue seeing the 22-year-old man.

Again Shirley took to sneaking out of her window at night to visit with him.

One afternoon, Shirley and her father got into a particularly nasty fight, and he told Shirley she wasn't to leave the house. Shirley stormed out anyway and ran straight to her welfare officer and showed a bruise on her arm, claiming that it was from her father. There was no going back. Shirley was removed from the care of her parents and placed under the care of welfare until the age of 18.

From then on Shirley was farmed out to foster homes, all the while refusing any contact with her family, despite their encouragement to do so and willingness to take her back home at any time that she said the word.

In 1958, Shirley and Des Finn were married in a registry office and the newlyweds returned to Des's home in Melbourne.

Shirley gave birth to their first son, Steven, seven weeks prematurely in 1959, followed by their second son, Shane, only one year later in 1960.

Shortly afterwards, Des was transferred from Melbourne to Perth with the RAAF, so the whole family relocated. Bridget, their third child, was born not long afterwards.

Life had been pretty good up until then but disaster struck. Des was seriously injured in an accident at work, leaving him partially castrated and as a result suffering from severe depression. Des was institutionalised for long periods of time at the Heathcote Mental Hospital, leaving Shirley with three very young children to care for, and no money to care for them with.

Shirley knew she had to do something to keep the bailiff at bay and put food on the table for her children. It was the 1960s and go-go dancers had become all the rage in the trendier nightclubs – young, attractive women in cages dancing for the enjoyment of the crowd, particularly the young men.

Shirley decided she'd give it a go, and donning a short skirt and long boots, set off to work at the Oasis Nightclub in Mount Hawthorn. She was a hit. Shirley soon made friends, one woman in particular, Sherryl, and she was popular with the gentlemen.

A photographer asked both Shirley and her friend to pose for some nude photographs for publication in overseas magazines. Excited, they agreed. Sherryl continued this modelling work to great success.

Things at home were still not going well. Des was out of hospital for a time, and encouraged Shirley to dabble in witchcraft. They met with a coven in Kings Park, along with some notable businessmen from the city. What had at first seemed like fun soon turned a little too dark for Shirley and she stopped going, much to Des's disappointment. This became another note of contention between the two in what was becoming an increasingly unhappy marriage.

The couple fought often, usually about money, and Des was known to be very abusive toward Shirley. She dreamt of getting away from it all and starting a whole new life but there didn't seem to be any way out.

Then Des was once again hospitalised for his depression. That was the straw that broke the camel's back for Shirley. Saddled with three children and a sick husband, she couldn't cope. Shirley took her children to the welfare office and handed them over into their care.

She joined the show circuit. All different kinds of acts toured with the Royal Agricultural Show: strong men, acrobats, fortune tellers and dancers. Shirley knew she could pull a crowd dancing, and she did. When she danced topless one night, the men went crazy and their show had never been busier. Shirley was given her own tent to perform in and continually pulled in big crowds; and even bigger ones when she had the idea of allowing men to paint her semi-naked body. Unfortunately for Shirley, as word spread of her show, so too did outrage and complaints and Shirley was forced to shut her show down and return home.

Des released himself from hospital and discovered what Shirley had done. He stormed into the welfare office and demanded his children back. They refused at first, but he wasn't taking no for an answer. Des took his children home where a repentant Shirley broke down in tears. Des swore that if she ever did anything like that again he would kill her.

Shirley and Des then started up a body painting and escort business on Albany Highway in Victoria Park, directly opposite the police station. They called it Regency Escorts and began to do good trade. There was talk of Shirley paying bribes to the police to ignore her business and allow her to continue operating.

In 1969, two police officers raided the premises and Shirley was horrified – she knew she had been green-lighted to continue operations. Still, she was convicted of 'keeping premises for the purpose of prostitution'.[11]

Shirley's conviction was reported in the newspaper and the family became social outcasts. None of their former associates, those of 'good moral standing' in the community wanted to know them anymore.

However, Shirley was forming strong connections of her own – with the police, and in particular the vice squad. She was one of only a select few brothel madams of the time given the go-ahead from police to operate. But there was a price.

Shirley's business grew and so did her name but trouble was brewing. The tax department had some serious questions about Shirley's finances, questions that she had no answers to.

After a trip to Singapore that Shirley was very excited about, calling it a business trip, large sums of money from a Hong Kong syndicate began to appear in her bank account. This money meant good things for Shirley's business but was ultimately a recipe for disaster.

***

Shirley and Des's marriage was all but over and it was decided that while Shirley concentrated on growing her ever-expanding business, Des would take the children to England to meet with family, and to give him some time to recuperate. Shirley financed the trip, writing to her children every week and sending them money. Once she even arrived unexpectedly as a surprise and took the children on a trip to Spain.

Shirley missed her children but she promised them that when they returned, life would be better; the business would be thriving and they'd never have to worry about money again. She was determined to keep that promise.

When the family returned two years later, Bridget, who by then was 10 years old, could barely believe her eyes. She knew her mother had promised to do well, but she could never have imagined what awaited her.

Shirley took them to their new home in South Perth, a massive federation-style house, with landscaped gardens, a sweeping driveway, a pool, and rooms filled with antique furniture. Shirley's dressing room was filled with designer clothing, and Bridget's own wardrobe was stuffed full of the most beautiful dresses her mother could buy.

In the garage was the most expensive Australian-made car of the time: a Dodge Phoenix.

Des was in need of a job so Shirley hired him to complete renovations on the new nightclub she'd purchased in Northbridge.

Workmen were nearly finished building the new pool, an extravagant piece fitted with solid gold tiles in its base, forming the initials SS – Shirley Shewring, her maiden name.

With businesses flourishing, Shirley looked set up for life, but unfortunately the tax man was closing in, demanding a bill of $100 000 in unpaid taxes. Shirley didn't have that kind of money, and besides, she said, she couldn't see why she should pay so much when such a huge sum of money was being shelled out every month in kick-backs and bribes to police and politicians. The tax man demanded to know who these alleged bribes were being paid to but Shirley said that to do so would put her in serious physical danger. She could neither reveal the names of those receiving bribes nor the identity of the true owner of the $73 000 held in a Hong Kong trust fund in Shirley's name.

Shirley was in a bind. If she didn't name names, she would be bankrupt and likely go to jail. If she did, she was in danger. It was a no-win situation.

On 23 June 1975, two days before Shirley was due to give evidence to the tax department, she was invited to an important business meeting with a mystery person. Apparently Shirley was expecting to be taken somewhere fancy as she dressed up in an expensive ball gown, one of her favourites, and dripping in $2000 worth of jewellery, awaited the mystery man to pick her up.

Bridget was told to stay in her room, and assuming that somebody would be there to look after her because there always was, she complied. Whether the mystery man arrived, or whether Shirley took off alone is still unknown.

The following morning, Bridget got up and went to her mother's room to wake her to take her to school. Her mother's bed was empty. Not knowing what to do, Bridget got herself ready and took herself to school. She couldn't have known there was anything wrong.

That day Shirley's Dodge Phoenix was spotted on a fairway of the Royal Perth Golf Course – a place police often used for meetings with informants. Inside, slumped across the seat, was Shirley Finn, still clad in her favourite dress, her jewellery untouched.

Shirley had been shot in the head four times, at close range, in what is known as a classic assassination style: the bowling ball. There was no doubt that somebody had wanted Shirley's body found and its whereabouts were a clear message.

***

Rumours about Shirley's death have swirled for years including the possible involvement of corrupt police officers, politicians and even other brothel madams. There were certainly plenty of people who would have benefited from her death. And even more who had reason to want to ensure her silence.

For a long time, people were reluctant to talk about Shirley's murder. Many of them knew what happened to Shirley, many knew about bribery and corruption in the police force in the 1970s, but they were all still too afraid for their own safety to talk. It seemed that Shirley's murderer got one thing right – the message was certainly heard, loud and clear.

However, in February 2014, the cold case of Shirley Finn's murder was reopened. The case was relaunched at the request of Shirley's daughter Bridget Shewring. In May 2015, it was reported that a former police officer claimed that he had seen Shirley Finn with two police detectives immediately prior to her death. WA Police Media released a statement that said in part, 'The investigation team has not received any advice or referrals from the Corruption and Crime Commission regarding any allegations by a former police officer. Further comment will not be made until the investigation [into the 1975 murder of Shirley Finn] is completed.'[12]

SIMONE VOGEL
16 September 1977

Her real name was Norma Pavich, but everyone knew her as Simone Vogel. In the 1960s, Simone worked in brothels in Sydney and had been one of the most trusted employees of Sydney vice king Joe Borg. When he turned the ignition in his car one day in 1968, sparking a car bomb that killed him instantly, Simone fled to Queensland.

She established a number of health studios, or massage parlours that everyone referred to as 'rub and tugs'. Simone did well, and opened six of these establishments over the next several years. Given the illegal nature of sex work, and the rampant corruption at the time of the Queensland police, it was no surprise that she paid for the privilege of being left alone by law enforcement.

Simone disappeared from her Brisbane home on 16 September 1977. On that day she was wearing $100 000 worth of jewellery and carrying $6000 in cash. She was allegedly on her way to meet with police who were standing over her. There was speculation that she had been murdered, and her body stuffed in the boot of her brand new Mercedes, and then driven over the border into New South Wales. Her car was found at Sydney airport 11 days later.

Simone's body was never found. She was officially declared dead on 7 July 1994.

ADELE BAILEY
September 1978

Adele Evelyn Bailey was a Pitcairn Islander who was born in Auckland, New Zealand in 1955. Adele was born a boy, Paul David Baily (she later added the 'e' to her surname), but knew from a very early age that she was female. She arrived in Australia in 1972, at the age of 17, and soon after had surgery for breast implants at Sydney Private Hospital. Her journey towards becoming a woman was underway. Four years later she travelled to Cairo where she underwent a number of full sex-change operations.

When she came back to Australia, Adele moved to Melbourne where she took up employment as a sex worker, both in parlours and on the streets of St Kilda. She was known to police for minor offences, but in general she was well-liked, and considered quiet, sweet and good-natured.

In 1978, she told friends in Adelaide she was coming to visit; however, she never turned up.

Almost 17 years later, two young men were fox hunting and fossicking on a property near Bonnie Doon in country Victoria. It was a property near the one owned by Detective Sergeant Denis Tanner. The boys discovered, down a disused mineshaft, bones and an odd assortment of clothes. They took a rib bone to a local doctor, who gave it a cursory examination and then called the police.

Police discovered that along with the bones were breast implants, a red woolly jumper, aqua knickers, cream woollen socks, high-heeled ankle boots, a small vanity mirror, a Timex watch and various pieces of costume jewellery.

It took the forensic anthropologist some time to put the pieces of the puzzle together. The long bones and the shape of the pelvis suggested the victim had been a man; the breast implants, clothes and jewellery hinted that the victim was female.

The mystery was solved when an Auckland family contacted police and told them Adele was missing. Dental records were sent over to the family dentist, and an identification was made.

All that was left of the young woman was bones, and the accompanying accessories. The breast implants and clothes suggested she might have been lying in the mineshaft since the 1970s. There was no way to determine the cause of death, or how long Adele Bailey had actually been dead.

During the police investigation, two former police detectives were questioned: Denis Tanner and Gerry McHugh. At a later inquest, Adele's sister spoke of a letter she had received in which Adele claimed she was in a relationship with Tanner. He denied it. More allegations came to light that the shack on the Bonnie Doon property was frequented by sex workers, and that Adele had been there for work.

Nobody has ever been charged with her murder. A $1 million reward remains on offer for anyone who has information leading to the arrest of a suspect in this case.

COLLEEN MOORE
4 November 1978

Colleen Moore, aged 25, was the mother of four young children. She was a sex worker who was based in Kings Cross. In the early hours of Saturday, 4 November 1978, she was seen entering a room of the Havilah Private Hotel in Sydney with a man. He was described as being about 30 years old, 183 centimetres tall, with a slim build, fair complexion, bent nose and dark wavy hair. He was wearing a light blue denim suit.

A newspaper seller in Darlinghurst Road, Bill Ninnes, saw the man come from the direction of the private hotel at about 3 a.m. He had blood on his hands, face and clothes – Ninnes thought he had been in a fight with someone. Police later learned that the man caught a taxi from Kings Cross to Lavender Street.

Colleen's bloodied body was discovered at around 4 a.m. Saturday morning in a blood-splattered bedroom. An ambulance was called but she was dead on arrival at St Vincent's Hospital. Colleen Moore had been beaten to death with a metal chair leg.

Her murder remains unsolved.

MARION SANDFORD
24 January 1980

Marion Sandford grew up in New Zealand. She trained to become a nurse, and it was during this time that she was introduced to heroin. Marion moved across the Tasman Sea to Sydney, Australia, where some of her family lived. She worked in Kings Cross to support her heroin habit, and became known to the police. At the age of 23 she had convictions related to heroin.

In January 1980, Marion was staying with her brother in the north shore suburb of Cammeray. She left him a note one morning saying that she would be gone for a few days, but Marion never returned home. When police investigated, they were told she had been approached to traffic drugs between Asia and Australia in exchange for thousands of dollars; however, there was no evidence that this had happened.

Police also feared there was a link between Marion's disappearance and that of two other women around the same time: aspiring model Linda Davie and nurse Mary Wallace.

In 2012, an inquest was conducted and Deputy State Coroner Paul MacMahon found that Marion may have died as a result of foul play. A $100 000 reward is on offer for information about the disappearance of Marion Sandford.

The Woman Who Knew Too Much
SALLIE-ANNE HUCKSTEPP
6 February 1986

There is little doubt that most of us have heard of Sallie-Anne Huckstepp, or think we know about her life – and more commonly her death. But for all that, Sallie-Anne was the epitome of the invisible woman. Her face may have been recognisable by anyone in the late 1980s when she turned whistleblower against police corruption and graced every news and current affairs show in Australia, but few knew the real Sallie-Anne.

In fact, it's doubtful that she even knew her real self.

Sallie-Anne wore many masks and was known by different people as various things: victim, prostitute, addict, whistleblower, gangster's moll, dog.

Sallie-Anne spent a lifetime courting danger and it all caught up with her in the end.

***

Sallie-Anne's childhood was not a happy one. Born Sallie-Anne Krivoshow, she grew up in Sydney's eastern suburbs, the eldest of two sisters in an unconventional Jewish family. Sallie-Anne's mother left when she was a small child, and her father often locked the little girl in a cupboard.

One friend, Cathy, later said, 'She had this really nice side to her which was really hard to say no to ... I don't know if any of her life was good, even from the age of two when her stepmother put a sign around her neck saying "I wet my bed" and made her walk up and down the street. Her childhood was a nightmare.'[13]

As a teenager, Sallie-Anne never fit in either. She attended, albeit fairly briefly, Moriah College – a Jewish school in Bellevue Hill – where she was the only girl who had blonde hair and whose father had no money. Sallie-Anne then went on to attend Dover Heights High School but she still wasn't like the other girls.

At 17, Sallie-Anne left school and married Bryan Huckstepp. Huckstepp was a petty criminal who Sallie-Anne had met through friends. He was exciting and dangerous and appealed to Sallie-Anne. Hopelessly in love, Sallie-Anne saw Huckstepp as her escape from the life that confined her. The two left Sydney and travelled to Kalgoorlie in Western Australia to live. Kalgoorlie is a small mining town with little to hold the interest of two young people; many of the residents are fly in–fly out workers who have no investment in the growth of the town. Bryan was a heroin addict and he asked Sallie-Anne to work as a prostitute, servicing the miners, to help pay for his habit. Sallie-Anne obliged and eventually developed her own heroin habit.

Bryan and Sallie-Anne moved back to Sydney where Sallie-Anne continued to earn money as a sex worker in the Kings Cross area. There she gave birth to a daughter and Sallie-Anne thought their new baby would be all the couple needed to get their lives back on track and make a real go of things. But it wasn't to be. Still unhappy, the two were unable to maintain their relationship and the marriage ended.

In 1981, Sallie-Anne met heroin dealer and standover man

Warren Lanfranchi and the two began a relationship. Lanfranchi was best known as working with the notorious criminal Arthur 'Neddy' Smith.

For a short time, Sallie-Anne discovered some true happiness with Lanfranchi. He helped straighten her out and she was clean of heroin for the first time in a long time. Friends say she was completely in love with him, and he with her. Their relationship was to last only four months though.

In June 1981, Lanfranchi, then just 22 years old, was lured to a meeting in Chippendale by Neddy Smith. When he arrived in the back alley of Dangar Place he was greeted by the corrupt Detective Sergeant Roger Rogerson and 17 other police officers.

'It's an ambush?' Lanfranchi asked.

'Yes, it is,' said Rogerson.[14]

He then shot Lanfranchi dead.

Rogerson maintained that Lanfranchi had pulled his weapon on him and he'd shot only in self-defence, but others, including and most vocally Sallie-Anne, said that Rogerson had wanted a $10 000 bribe.

Rogerson was never charged with Lanfranchi's murder; in fact, he received a bravery award for his conduct. However, he was later dismissed in disgrace from the police force when other allegations of corruption were proved to be true.

Lanfranchi's murder would bring Sallie-Anne to the attention of the whole of Australia. For the first three months following his death, grieving and afraid for her own life, she went into hiding. Then something snapped. Why should they get away with it? For years she'd been paying bribes to corrupt police to keep her liberty and to be able to work. For years police in New South Wales had been green-lighting crime to those willing and able to pay for it, and stitching up those who weren't. And now they'd murdered her boyfriend and she knew it. Sallie-Anne decided to talk.

On 15 July 1981, Sallie-Anne, accompanied by her father, Jack Krivoshow, and a Legal Aid solicitor, went to the New South Wales Police Headquarters in College Street, Darlinghurst. There she met with Detective Inspector Ralph and Detective Reith of the NSW Internal Affairs branch. The statement she made would eventually help lead to the end of corruption in the New South Wales Police Department, by way of the Independent Commission Against Corruption, and the Wood Royal Commission.

Her statement in part said:

I will tell you everything ... I have the following criminal record: I have 31 convictions for prostitution. I have a conspiracy to defraud conviction which occurred shortly after I left Harry Bailey's tender care at 'Chelmsford'. I then had two further marijuana convictions. A heroin conviction when I was loaded up by Detectives Peter and Tomich at the Lido bar. I have a further 'use' charge in which moneys were paid to the police to effect the outcome ... While operating as a prostitute I made regular payments to members of the Vice Squad over ten years. I have been involved in a number of transactions which I referred to in my statement which have involved substantial payment to members of the Drug Squad and other detectives relating to drug matters. I believe that the New South Wales Drug Squad and the Armed Hold-Up Squad are both totally corrupt and that they feed on the very activities which they are supposed to stop.[15]

And Sallie-Anne didn't stop there. She went to the media and gave extensive interviews where she made allegations of Rogerson's involvement in Lanfranchi's death and other police corruption.

Australia fell in love with Sallie-Anne's quick wit, intelligence and beauty. She became the darling of Australian media.

It's not hard to see why she came across so well on television when you look at the answers she gave when questioned during the inquest into Lanfranchi's death. Brian Murphy, QC for Rogerson, asked Sallie-Anne about Lanfranchi's use of violence:

Q: Incidentally, on one of these drug rip-offs, did he tell you that he'd forced someone into the boot of a car and locked them in there?

A: Yes, he did.

Q: Be a lot easier to do with a gun, wouldn't it?

A: I don't, well, I've never forced anyone into the boot of a car, Mr Murphy. Have you?

Q: Did he carry a baseball bat?

A: I have seen a baseball bat in the car on one occasion, yes.

Q: Did he tell you what he used the baseball bat for?

A: Mr Murphy, he wasn't dealing with respectable citizens, he was dealing with criminals and junkies.[16]

The adoration of the public lent Sallie-Anne a different kind of addiction and she was able to wean herself off heroin for a while and dream of a different kind of life. She appeared on *60 Minutes* and other current affairs shows, a documentary was made about her life, Penguin gave her an advance to write a book, and for six months she wrote for *Penthouse* magazine. The editor there described her as a 'natural writer'.

What Sallie-Anne couldn't see was how far she was alienating the people she knew. Not everybody was happy with the stories Sallie-Anne was telling.

By early 1985, Sallie-Anne was drawn right back to her roots, beginning a relationship with a 33-year-old drug dealer, David Kelleher, who had recently been released from prison. Sallie-Anne described him as her 'big blond god', exactly the kind of muscle-bound man she had always been drawn to. It was as if Sallie-Anne just couldn't help herself. No matter how much life outside the criminal world was good to her, she was always drawn back to the dark side.

One close friend said, 'She was a gangster's moll, she couldn't help herself. That's how she got her buzz in life, it was almost more than the dope itself.'[17]

Sallie-Anne moved into an expensive apartment with Kelleher and her then 12-year-old daughter.

When this boyfriend disappeared without so much as a goodbye, Sallie-Anne was stuck. She couldn't afford the apartment alone and went back to sex work to pay the bills. She also began dealing in small amounts of heroin, organised with a friend who would sell it on the streets.

Sallie-Anne, her dealer friend and Sallie-Anne's daughter left the apartment and began what was quite a transient existence for some time, moving from one cheap hotel to the next.

David Kelleher reappeared on the scene for a brief time, but only long enough to be arrested by the Australian Federal Police for the importation of $2.2 million worth of heroin.

Sallie-Anne then began yet another relationship with a criminal, this time a man who turned state's evidence in a big drug case and had to spend time in a Federal Police safe house. During his time there, the safe house was burgled and a number of fur coats, said to belong to a Federal Police inspector, were stolen, along with some video equipment. The theft was a huge embarrassment to the Federal Police, some would say out of all proportion to their actual value.

One informant posited, 'They didn't care about the furs. They wanted the contents. What's in the lining? It must have been dope for the coppers to be running around looking for it.'[18]

And Sallie-Anne was right in the middle of it all again. When Kelleher was found for questioning, he was with Sallie-Anne but denied any knowledge of the burglary. However, the police used Sallie-Anne's intimate knowledge of the drug and crime scene in Sydney to help them look for the stolen furs.

A friend said, 'She was running so hot. She was driving around the Cross with the Federal Police, two car loads of Federal Police, looking for these furs. She even went out to Long Bay with them … Word goes right around the jail in about 20 seconds flat that she's a dog. She's hanging out with all these Federal coppers and they're probably supporting her habit at the same time.'[19]

Distrust of Sallie-Anne was rife in the criminal underworld, though she maintained that she was in fact using the Feds to help Kelleher. She said that they'd made offers to help him out if she helped them. She also came up with plans to blackmail the police into helping him. 'She thought she could do a bit of blackmail by trying to suggest improper dealings with the police and set them up and have it taped,' said a friend.[20]

At this point, Sallie-Anne's daughter had had enough. She moved away to live with her father.[21]

Sallie-Anne was indeed courting danger. She embarked on a new relationship with a Federal Police officer, further compromising herself in the eyes of her criminal associates.

There was talk on both sides that either she was using the policeman to help Kelleher, or that she was planning to inform on Kelleher. One thing was clear – Sallie-Anne could no longer be trusted by either side.

To Sallie-Anne though, dating Federal Police officer Peter Parker Smith was like a breath of fresh air. She could hardly believe that life could be turned around so completely; for the first time she felt like she was on the right side of the law.

Sallie-Anne's friend said she 'was swinging from one side to another. She didn't know where she was going. She kept saying in one breath she was doing all this stuff to help Kelleher, and in the next breath she's talking about giving him up. Then she's on with this cop. Sallie-Anne lived in a fantasy world, she kept thinking no one believed she was a dog.'[22]

Sallie-Anne was wiped by everyone, even the woman who had long been selling heroin for her on the streets. She had no heroin supplier and no dealers. And no friends.

At this point Sallie-Anne began to seriously fear for her safety. Reality had finally kicked in, Sallie-Anne's fantasy world gradually melted away and she realised the predicament she'd put herself in. She penned a letter in December 1985 to her ex-husband, Bryan Huckstepp: 'Look after [our daughter] for me if something goes wrong – I don't want to seem depressive, but I think you'll have to look after her – I may not be able to make any choices for myself in the near future. Give her all my love, always, Sallie-Anne. xxxx'[23]

Three days after Christmas, on 28 December, Sallie-Anne was on her way to meet a new heroin supplier in Ashfield. Having always been a wild driver, Sallie-Anne lost control of her car and, at about 9 p.m., rolled her car on Cleveland Street. Her arm was badly broken, requiring surgery, and Sallie-Anne spent a week in hospital.

Following her discharge from hospital in mid-January, yet another of Sallie-Anne's relationships came to an end and she moved into a flat in Woollahra with an old friend, Tom, and his flatmate Gwendoline Beecroft, whom Sallie-Anne hadn't met before.

Sallie-Anne dreamt – yet again – of starting afresh. Perhaps life with a 'straight cop' was a means of escaping her struggle with using and dealing drugs. Maybe she could start writing again; she'd been good at that and enjoyed it.

Her relationship with Peter Parker Smith flourished and he would often drop around to the flat, or she would go and spend the night with him. She told Tom, 'I can't believe it, I've fallen in love with a Federal policeman. Now for the first time since Warren, it's happening with a police officer, someone who almost stands for what took him away from me.'[24]

But not everyone was so optimistic about Sallie-Anne's future, nor certainly her relationship with Peter, not the least of whom was her new dealer, Warren Richards.

Richards was a former Olympic judo champion but was better known on the streets as a hard man, friend to the notorious Arthur 'Neddy' Smith, and part of a drug syndicate known as 'the Untouchables' who were known for their skills at intimidation.

One police informant said of him, 'When the police catch you, they lock you up. When Warren catches you, he'll put a bullet in you.'[25]

Richards was more than a little concerned about Sallie-Anne's relationship with Peter Parker Smith. Apparently he'd been told by one of his police contacts that Sallie-Anne had been spilling information on him to Parker Smith.

A friend of Sallie-Anne's confided, 'He was furious. He was screaming abuse saying, "I don't care if she's a friend of yours. She's a dog."'[26]

Sallie-Anne became increasingly frightened of Richards, with Tom and Gwendoline noticing the change in their flatmate. Gwendoline said later that Sallie-Anne seemed happy at first to receive Richards' calls but then something changed. 'She was being harassed. In the last two weeks I could feel it in the air. My house took on a bad atmosphere.'[27] Gwendoline caught Sallie-Anne injecting heroin between her toes in the bathroom and told her that was enough, she had enough stress in her life without all this, she'd have to go. Move out. Sallie-Anne started crying. She had nowhere else to go.

On 4 February 1986, Sallie-Anne arrived home at about 4 p.m. and changed into an apricot camisole that she liked to wear around the house. She settled in by the window and subconsciously rubbed at her injured arm. It still seemed to be causing her a good deal of pain.

Tom came home, grabbed some shirts and left again. Sallie-Anne suggested to Gwendoline that they have a quiet night in and that she wasn't expecting a phone call until about five to 11 that night. Gwendoline cooked dinner and ducked out for a bottle of wine. When she returned, after about 10 minutes, Sallie-Anne was relaxed and painting her nails.

After dinner, Gwendoline went to bed but was woken up at 10.55 by the ringing of the phone. The man on the other end said, 'Is Sallie-Anne there?' Gwendoline handed the phone to Sallie-Anne who had just hopped out of the shower, wrapping herself in a towel.

Sallie-Anne's relaxed mood changed immediately and she began running around frantically to get ready. 'It's Wozza [Warren Richards],' she explained to Gwendoline. 'At least I haven't got to go to Ashfield this time.'[28]

Sallie-Anne threw on a blue top and a pair of jeans and flew out the door, only to bound back up the stairs moments later, brushing past Gwendoline in the doorway and running first to her bedroom, and then to pull apart the cushions on the couch. Panicky, she said, 'My keys. I've forgotten my bloody keys.'[29]

Gwendoline was worried. It wasn't like Sallie-Anne to be so frantic, so stressed. Sallie-Anne once again ran for the door, calling out to Gwendoline that she'd be back in five to 10 minutes. Gwendoline went to the front window to watch Sallie-Anne leave, but saw nothing. Not even her car pulling away. She went back to bed not knowing that that was to be the last time anyone would see Sallie-Anne alive.

At 10.30 the following morning, Friday, 7 February 1986, a dog walker in Centennial Park noticed a body floating in Busby Pond. He immediately called the police who pulled the body from the water. As soon as her face was visible, one of the policemen recognised her: 'That's Huckstepp.'

A post-mortem examination revealed that Sallie-Anne had been strangled and drowned in Busby Pond.

***

Theories abounded about who Sallie-Anne's killer might be, from Kelleher wanting revenge for her apparent disloyalty, to the most commonly held belief that Warren Richards and Neddy Smith had her killed because she'd become too much of a liability to them.

No evidence was found to link anybody, with any certainty, to Sallie-Anne's death though.

In 1987, an inquest into Sallie-Anne's death began. It was one of Australia's longest inquests, spanning over four years. At the inquest a recording was played where Neddy Smith confessed to a cellmate in Long Bay Correctional Centre. He was recorded saying he'd attacked Sallie-Anne from behind as she arrived at

Centennial Park, punched her, grabbed her by the throat, lifted her off the ground and then strangled her for about six minutes. He then claimed to have dragged the defenceless woman to the pond where he held her head under water for several more minutes.

This certainly tied in with the coronial evidence surrounding her murder.

In the recording, Smith said, 'Strangling somebody is the hardest thing in the world … but the most satisfying thing I ever did in my life.'[30]

However, Smith later denied his own confession, stating that he knew he was being recorded and he had lied to gain publicity for his new book.

Smith was subsequently charged with Sallie-Anne's murder but was acquitted in 1999. Smith fuelled the allegations and rumours that disgraced detective Roger Rogerson was responsible for Sallie-Anne's death in retribution for his failing career and outing as a corrupt police officer. Smith went on to discuss the matter in an interview with author John Dale saying that Sallie-Anne was murdered 'because she kept bugging Roger, ringing him up and leaving messages that he was a dog … The reason they didn't bury her or dispose of her body was Roger wanted her left floating in the pond as a message. The bloke who killed her has never been arrested and is not in jail.'[31]

Nobody has yet been prosecuted of the murder of Sallie-Anne Huckstepp. Her death remains a mystery.

LILLIAN LORENZ
26 September 1986

Lillian Bridget Lorenz's body was found in the Brisbane River with a severe blow to the back of her head. Her murder has never been solved.

CHERYL BURCHELL
22 April 1987

Cheryl Burchell had been on methadone for two years. At the age of 28, she was working hard to turn her life around and had reached a point where she was only soliciting part-time to earn money when she wanted something special. Cheryl lived in Mayfield, a suburb of Newcastle in New South Wales, and on the night of 22 April 1987, she went out to work the Maitland Road strip. She told friends she was saving up for a holiday.

The following morning at about 9 a.m., three schoolboys discovered her body on the banks of Throsby Creek. When police arrived they saw drag marks and bloodstains near the long grass, and debris near the bank of the creek. Cheryl had her own bra twisted around her neck. It had been used to strangle her. She also had several stab wounds on her back, neck and chest.

It was 24 years later that forensic technology was able to isolate skin cells from her bra and develop a DNA profile. However, Cheryl Burchell's murder remains unsolved, and there is a $50 000 reward for information that may lead to an arrest.

JODIE LARCOMBE
December 1987

Jodie Maree Larcombe was 21 and working as a street-based sex worker in St Kilda. She'd been on the streets for about two years. Jodie was a regular heroin user and dabbled in other drugs. Friends saw her in November 1987 just before she spent a short time in prison for a minor offence. She was released on 22 December 1987.

Police are not even sure when she went missing, such was the transient nature of her life, but they know it was sometime between December 1987 and March 1988. Friends recall seeing her on Boxing Day, but that is the last time Jodie was seen alive.

Darryl Suckling was 50 years old and the caretaker of a property in south-west NSW. He spent time in Melbourne and got to know Jodie. According to him, they were friends of sorts. So when Jodie went missing, police looked at Suckling as a suspect, and their interest sharpened when they learned Suckling had left Melbourne on 27 December to return to his isolated property. Police searched the property and found a purple dress and deodorant, which Suckling later asked his sister to tell the police were hers. Police also located Jodie's dental plate in Suckling's truck.

Suckling was arrested in April 1989 for Jodie's murder but the charges were dropped in October 1990 due to a lack of evidence.

In 1992, Suckling was sent to prison for unrelated charges. Following his release, police convinced an ex-cellmate of Suckling to wear a wire. The man revealed to police that Suckling had told him he had killed Jodie and was planning to abduct another woman. Among the many incriminating words that can be heard on the recording, Suckling said, 'I got away with fucken murder ... I'm laughing at the coppers because they know I've done it and can't prove it.'[32]

Suckling went to trial in 1996 and was found guilty and sentenced to serve life in prison. He lodged several appeals, all of which were unsuccessful.

Jodie Larcombe's mother, Dot, committed suicide on the day Suckling lodged his appeal to the High Court in 1999.

CARY-JANE PIERCE
2 October 1988

Cary-Jane Louise Pierce left her mother's home in Wambool Street, Bulimba, an outer suburb of Brisbane, at around 10.25 p.m. on 17 September 1988. A little over two weeks later she was found dead in bushland near the Gateway Bridge in Brisbane's eastern suburbs. She had been battered around the head with large rocks, and a strap from the canvas knapsack she was carrying was bound tightly around her neck. Her murder has never been solved. Queensland Police have offered a reward of $250 000 for information that leads to the arrest and conviction of her killer.

ROSLYN HAYWARD
13 September 1990

Roslyn Hayward's partially clothed body was found covered in ti tree and bracken just off a bush track in Sorrento, Victoria, on 13 September 1990.

Roslyn was a 30-year-old mother of two young children, aged only eight and two years old at the time of her murder.

She had been hired by a man named Gregory John Brazel in the early hours of Thursday, 13 September 1990, for the purposes of sex. He then lured her back to his apartment for further services. Brazel drugged Roslyn with chlorpromazine, strangled her and then disposed of her body.

Brazel was on an early release program from prison for several violent crimes including armed robbery and arson, and had only been a free man for eight months at the time he met with Roslyn.

Brazel was convicted of Roslyn's murder and is currently serving time in jail for that and two other murders.

SHARON TAYLOR
23 September 1990

Sharon Taylor was, above all else, the devoted mother of a little girl, just four years old at the time of her mother's death. Sharon had her daughter's name tattooed on her body, and despite a lifestyle which included drug dependence and sex work, she shielded her young daughter from it all, allowing her to grow with the innocence she should.

Sharon ran a small escort agency from Geelong and on 28 May 1990, her services were engaged for a client: Gregory John Brazel.

On 23 September 1990, Sharon's naked body was discovered in a shallow grave at Barangarook, south of Colac in Victoria. She had been stabbed five times – four of those through the heart.

Brazel is currently serving three jail terms for the murders of Sharon, another sex worker Roslyn Hayward (see previously), and Mordialloc hardware shop owner Mildred Hanmer. He will be eligible for parole in 2020.

AMANDA BYRNES
7 April 1991

Amanda Byrnes was a 23-year-old sex worker who worked in St Kilda, Melbourne. Witnesses saw Amanda either get into, or be dragged into, a vehicle that may have been a Morris 850 panel van, white or off-white, around midnight. It side-swiped a parked car and swerved wildly as she fought, her legs protruding from an open door. Six hours later her naked body was found on the foreshore at Elwood. Amanda had been stabbed and beaten.

Her murder has never been solved.

SUZANNE GRANT
28 May 1991

Suzanne Grant was a 21-year-old mother of a young baby. Her body was found in Greenbank, Queensland. She met a brutal death – she was strangled, stabbed and then set alight on a rubbish tip. Her head and upper body were wrapped in plastic, and her hands and legs were bound together.

Suzanne's murderer has not been found.

Mail-Order Aside
PIA NAVIDA
31 January 1992

The mail-order bride business was a thriving one in the late 1970s and the 1980s. Women desperate to escape extreme poverty, particularly in countries like Thailand and the Philippines, saw marriage to an Australian as their best chance at a better life.

Australia was prosperous; the promised land of opportunity, education, employment and money. Lots of money. Certainly the Australian men who frequented the organised sex tours of these countries seemed to have plenty of money to splash around.

For some men, it was an opportunity to find love, find a wife and start a family of their own. Many had been unable to attract the attentions of an Aussie girl, and still many more were older and divorced or widowed, with few prospects for future happiness. They willingly responded to the advertisements placed by women, tempting men to marry them and bring them 'home' to Australia.

For other men though, the motivations were a little less pure. For some the prospect of a subservient wife, a woman desperate enough to escape her situation that she'd put up with anything, was the drawcard. Horrendous tales of domestic abuse have unfolded, of women used as nothing more than slaves to meet the whims, both domestically and sexually, of a domineering husband. Many of these men became known as serial husbands, dumping one wife and trading her for another, usually younger, bride when his attractions waned. The future of his previous wife was no longer his concern; she would be cut adrift with no friends, no family and no money with which to support herself.

For other women the future was even more bleak. The Centre for Philippines Concerns – Australia reports at least 35 documented cases involving the deaths or suspicious disappearances of Filipino women and children since the 1980s.

For teenage Pia Navida, marriage to an Australian man was like the culmination of all her dreams come true. She would escape the poverty and back-breaking work of her life in the Philippines. Pia imagined a nice house in the suburbs, a future she would have with chances of a good education for the children, and enough money to not only buy herself nice things – new clothes, jewellery and items to furnish her imagined home – but also enough money to send home to her mother and sister she'd left behind, to make their lives a little easier. Perhaps one day she could even bring them to live in Australia too.

Reality rarely lives up to the dream. Pia's marriage to the Australian man who brought her here in 1983 was short-lived. Like so many mail-order brides before her, Pia, who could speak little English, found herself stranded in a strange place with almost no usable skills. She had no family and no friends from whom to seek guidance, and no way of knowing where to find any of the help that may have been available to her.

Pia believed she was alone and would have to find her own way to survive in this country that had held so much promise.

It wasn't long before Pia realised that her most valuable commodity was her body. Just like at home in the Philippines, men were always available, and they were only too willing to engage her services for sex.

Pia never really had a place to call home in Australia. She lived quite a nomadic lifestyle, moving from place to place searching for that something that would remind her of the all-but-forgotten dreams she'd had before moving to Australia.

As she moved from state to state, trading sex for money and a place to stay, Pia always managed to fall in with the 'wrong' crowd – the kind of people who could see how vulnerable Pia was and took advantage of that. When things got too bad she would move away again, to start fresh in a new town, in another part of the country. But no matter where she went, always the same kind of people. And the sex work. And the drugs.

Pia developed a serious heroin habit, pushing her into that endless cycle of needing drugs to sustain the demands of the sex work, and needing the work to sustain the drug habit. It also meant that the types of people she associated with became increasingly unsavoury.

It seemed almost inevitable that Pia would wind up in Sydney, staying in various motels and boarding houses around Central Station near Kings Cross. Here, it seems, Pia finally found herself something akin to a home, a place where she had some sense of belonging, though it was a far cry from the lifestyle she'd imagined as a poor girl in the Philippines.

By now Pia had developed the street smarts necessary for a woman in her trade, and was known within her circle of friends as being somebody who could look after herself.

Pia entered a volatile, and often violent, relationship with a local man named Wayne Taylor. The two were known to frequent a cafe in Surry Hills called Greasies, commonly used as a drug-dealing haunt.

Most of Pia's increasingly large group of friends knew they

could find Pia at Greasies, on her usual patch where she solicited for work, or at a hotel in Pitt Street where she often lived and regularly took clients.

Pia didn't take unnecessary risks and would never go with a client to an unknown location, so when on 31 January 1992, 37-year-old Pia disappeared, her friends were worried.

Just before midday the following morning, two bushwalkers, Joseph Cassidy and his girlfriend, Nicole Lamaro, were walking a fire trail in the Royal National Park, south of Sydney. Cassidy first came across items that he described as the contents of a woman's handbag strewn across the ground. As they continued to walk further along the trail, he saw a pair of women's knickers. Alert now, Cassidy and Lamaro looked more carefully as they walked. They observed blood on a large rock, and then what they described as 'drag marks' that led off the track and into an area of bushland. Cassidy followed the drag marks and came upon the naked body of a female, her head covered in dried blood. A glass-beaded necklace was wrapped around her left hand. Cassidy and Lamaro called the police who quickly cordoned off the area and began collecting evidence.

The body was later identified as being that of Pia Navida.

Samples were taken from the rock which was presumed, and later confirmed, to be the murder weapon, and swabs were taken from Pia's body.

Detectives began an exhaustive investigation, which included examining tyre marks found near the site, but found little. Wayne Taylor, who Pia had had such a tumultuous relationship with, was vigorously investigated but eventually cleared.

The trail was cold; police had no further leads.

An inquest in 2004 returned an open finding. Only Pia and her killer or killers knew what happened and they weren't talking. So the case remained unsolved, police had new cases to worry about and people got on with their lives. Pia was almost forgotten – just another soul lost to the harsh life of a drug addict and sex worker in Sydney.

Her killers must have thought they'd literally gotten away with murder.

***

In 2008, almost two decades after Pia's death, New South Wales police instigated a new team of detectives dedicated to investigating cold cases. With major developments in DNA and forensic technology in the past few years, and with the chance that so many years after a crime, witnesses, and often even the perpetrators themselves, might be more willing to talk, a cold case unit was established to clear some of the backlog of unsolved cases in New South Wales. Some 420 homicides had remained unsolved in New South Wales since 1975. One of those was Pia Navida. So when Pia's file landed on the desks of the new task force, the case was reopened and police were finally able to piece together the puzzle of Pia's death and arrest a suspect.

Police scoured the earlier reports and ascertained that a 14-kilogram rock found near the body and covered in blood was the murder weapon.

According to the autopsy, the injuries sustained included a laceration to the area behind Pia's ear, typical of one caused by impact with a blunt object, extensive abrasions and grazing of her entire head and forehead, and also her right shoulder, back of her trunk and her hip consistent with having been dragged by the arms over a rough surface. There were fractures to one rib and the base and top of the skull consistent with impact with a large heavy object. The autopsy concluded that the cause of Pia's death was the head injuries, most likely sustained by multiple blows to the head with the rock.

Next, police turned to the samples taken from Pia's body, including semen found in her vagina, anus and on her body, and fingernail clippings. They sent these samples for DNA testing using newer technology than was available in 1992. The samples matched three different men: Steve Isac Matthews, Rodney James Paterson and a third unknown man. Neither of the men named had been interviewed back in 1992 so police knew they had the breakthrough they needed.

Both Matthews and Paterson initially denied having ever seen Pia before but were unable to provide any reason why their DNA might be found on her body and under her fingernails. Both men were arrested for murder.

The case against Matthews was compelling, and despite his initial denials, he changed his plea to one of guilty just before the trial was set to commence.

Matthews stated that a head injury he sustained from a major assault in 2005 had led to a loss of memory so that he was very vague about the circumstances surrounding Pia's death. Medical experts refuted the claim, saying the type of injury Matthews had received shouldn't have that kind of memory loss, but Justice Geoffrey Bellew accepted this as the reason for his earlier denials and for being unable to testify against his co-accused Paterson, or provide any information about the third man.

Matthews did agree to the prosecution's order of events surrounding Pia's death: Pia was taken against her will by Matthews and two other men to the Royal National Park, an area that Matthews used to camp in as a child and was well-acquainted with. She was then raped both vaginally and anally by all three men, one at a time, the other two holding her down against her struggles.

Friends of Pia testified to the fact that Pia wouldn't willingly 'do anal' and would certainly fight back against any attacker, as was indicated by the DNA found under her fingernails. Pia's fight wasn't enough against three strong men though. When they'd finished the sexual attack, Matthews raised a large rock, found nearby, and struck Pia several times in the head. Even as she screamed, blood coursing down her face from the massive wound in her head from the first hit, he raised the rock again, smashing it into her skull.

Matthews' ex-girlfriend Nicole Duffin gave evidence that Matthews often took her for picnics in bushland near where Pia's body was found. On one such occasion he told Duffin that he'd killed someone nearby and then demonstrated how, with two hands, he'd smashed a rock down onto the victim's head.

A drug addict with a fairly extensive criminal history, both before and after Pia's murder, of crimes related to dishonesty, Matthews nonetheless had no form for other violent acts. The sentencing judge considered this and accepted Matthews' statement that he was 'disgusted and sickened' by his actions and was genuinely remorseful.

However, the severity of the crime called for a severe sentence and Matthews received a total of 21 years and six months imprisonment for Pia's murder. He will be eligible for parole in 2027.

The case against co-accused Rodney Paterson was not so clear-cut, and he certainly wasn't going to confess.

Paterson was found to have lied between police interviews, first saying he didn't know Pia or Matthews, but then later admitting that he travelled to Queensland with Matthews and another unnamed man early in 1992 – after Pia's death.

Paterson frequented Greasies and admitted that he would most likely have known Pia and her then boyfriend Wayne

Taylor: 'I probably sold to them or I would have seen them if they were there.'[33]

He could not however provide a reason for how his semen came to be found in Pia's rectal cavity, or his DNA under her fingernails.

This mystery was solved when police listened to a conversation they recorded of him and his partner. He told her, 'She kept comin' around to the corner when I was drinkin' with Lucy and that, I met her through Tracy, that other broad. Probably I slept with her probably 10 times over a six-week period.'[34]

Eventually he admitted that he'd had consensual sex with Pia and that the last time they'd been together he'd left her asleep in the back of his panel van. It was also possible, he said, that it was around the same day she was murdered. His excuse for not telling police earlier? He didn't want to bring himself into it and it was only a '50/50 chance that my DNA would pop up'.[35]

However, all the evidence against Paterson was purely circumstantial and the fact that he'd had sex with Pia within 48 hours of her death wasn't enough to come to the conclusion that he'd been involved in her murder. There was also no way of concluding that the sex was anything other than consensual.

Justice Bellew directed the jury to return a verdict of not guilty on all counts – murder, manslaughter and aggravated sexual assault – due to a lack of evidence. Rodney Paterson is a free man.

The third offender is still unknown and remains, for now, at large. Perhaps more advances in technology will help bring this killer to justice. Or perhaps his accomplice will miraculously recover his memory of that day and give the police a name. It's doubtful either way that this killer will ever rest easy again.

MELISSA RYAN
1 May 1993

Melissa Jane Ryan was a 21-year-old outcall sex worker who lived, worked and ultimately died on the Gold Coast in Queensland. She took a booking to meet a client at the Sun Valley Motel in Currumbin in Queensland. When Melissa met with him on 1 May 1993, she was stabbed to death. After an intensive investigation, police charged Charles Sewell with her murder. He was convicted in court.

MICHELLE COPPING
1 February 1994

Michelle Copping was the mother of a three-year-old boy. She was a 26-year-old woman who worked on the streets of St Kilda. Michelle was last seen getting into a red Commodore taxi.

On Tuesday, 1 February 1994, Michelle's naked body was found in a laneway behind a house off Barkly Street. Police speculated she may have been run over by the person who beat and strangled her. Michelle's murder remains unsolved.

KERRIE PANG
14 February 1994

Kerrie Pang was the 36-year-old manager of Kerrie's Oasis, a massage parlour in Gladesville, Sydney. On the evening of Valentine's Day 1994, she arrived at work to join her 25-year-old employee, Fatma Ozanal. Police became aware of a crime when firefighters were called to a blaze at the address, and discovered two women inside the premises. It quickly became obvious they hadn't died in the fire. Fatma Ozanal had been shot, and Kerrie Pang had been shot and then stabbed repeatedly in the neck, face and chest.

It was a long investigation and police focused on Kerrie's partner, Mark Lewis, who managed a massage parlour in Ryde. However, it wasn't until a man called Ronald Waters came forward to police that the case was solved. He revealed he was paid $600 by a man named Lindsay Robert Rose to help him kill Pang and Ozanal, and that the murder had been organised and paid for by Kerrie Pang's partner, Mark Lewis.

Rose was a contract killer, yet the way Kerrie Pang had been murdered – being shot, then stabbed repeatedly – suggested that he was more than that. In fact, Kerrie Pang was a former girlfriend of his. Because Kerrie would have recognised Rose, he had needed Robert Waters' help to gain access to her workplace. During Mark Lewis's trial, evidence indicated that the motives for the murders had been problems in Lewis and Kerrie's relationship, and Lewis's dissatisfaction with Kerrie's line of work, as well as Rose's hatred of Kerrie Pang.

In 1998, Lindsay Robert Rose was convicted of five murders and sentenced to life in prison without the possibility of parole. In 2000, Mark Lewis was sentenced to life in prison for the murder of Kerry Pang, and 18 years for the killing of Fatma Ozanal. Ronald Waters was found guilty of being an accessory to murder and was sentenced to 18 months' periodic detention.

SAMANTHA MIZZI
30 March 1994

Samantha Louisa Mizzi was a 23-year-old mother who moved to Melbourne from Maldon in central Victoria. She worked the streets of St Kilda until one Saturday night, when a fellow worker found her naked and terribly injured. She was lying in bushes at the back of a car park behind an office building in Blanche Street, St Kilda. She was rushed to the Alfred Hospital where she died 10 hours later from severe head injuries. Her skull had been fractured.

Police investigated but found little at the scene. Her clothes and personal belongings were never found, and there was no sign of a weapon. Samantha's murder has not been solved.

She's a Beautiful Dancer
REVELLE BALMAIN
5 November 1994

In some ways it is the most devastating kind of loss when someone you love vanishes and there is no explanation. No resolution. All you have are clues, hints and the scuttlebutt of what people think might have happened. You fear the worst, hope for the best, rack your brain for answers. *Where could she be? Why hasn't she called me? Why won't she come home?*

Fear, the kind that gnaws away at the lining of your stomach, holds you hostage. Disbelief helps you keep grief at bay, until it becomes impossible to ignore. She got lost. She decided to take some time out and she'll be home any day now, she met someone she didn't want to tell us about and ran off with them. She's hurt, she's lying somewhere and can't get help.

All the while a nagging voice in the back of your mind is whispering, *She's dead. She hasn't called anyone. She hasn't touched her bank account. She's not the kind of girl who'd walk away ... she would never put you through this kind of pain.*

You hear on the news that bushwalkers have found a body. You hold your breath. Your gut clenches with equal measures of terror and hope. Until you know – it isn't her.

Then your mind starts to haunt you. Where is she? Did she

suffer? You look with envy, even resentment when families of murder victims bury their loved ones, bring them home. Then you feel guilty, you understand their suffering. But you've got nothing. No child, no body, no story to help you know what happened, how they left you. Or why.

You're in limbo.

***

Jan Balmain had been a dancer and a teacher. She used to run her own dance school on the Northern Beaches of Sydney. And for a while the life she shared with her husband, Ivor, was wonderful. She had three children: Suellen, her daughter from an earlier marriage, Revelle and Matthew.

It all changed one morning when her four-year-old daughter, Revelle, ran inside to tell her Matthew was in the pool. Jan raced outside to discover their 15-month-old baby lifeless in the family's swimming pool.

Revelle became the focus of Jan and Ivor's life. She went to a private school, and learned ballet, tap and jazz. She was growing into a beautiful young woman: tall, willowy and blonde. When she was still a teenager she talked to her mother about her future, and told her she wanted to be a professional dancer.

Jan was thrilled. She got in touch with people she knew, and through a friend, helped her daughter get a contract performing in hotels in Japan. Revelle spent 18 months in Japan, dancing and gaining more experience, after which time she returned to Sydney.

On the surface at least, Revelle Balmain's star was on the rise. It was 1994, and the 22-year-old was by now an accomplished dancer. More recently she had added modelling to her portfolio. She had done a photoshoot for *Oyster* magazine, and her face would soon grace its cover.

Towards the end of 1994, Revelle told her mother she was going back to Japan for another six-month stint dancing in a cabaret show. She had to go to Brisbane for two weeks' rehearsals before heading overseas. She wanted to see her family before she left, so she organised to catch the train to Newcastle on Sunday, 6 November. She told her mother she would catch the 9.30 a.m. train from Sydney.

That morning her mother arrived at the Newcastle Railway Station in plenty of time to meet the 11 a.m. train, while Ivor stayed at home making lunch for the family. However, Revelle was not on the train. At first Jan was perplexed that her daughter hadn't arrived, and she tried to contact her to see what had happened. She waited for the next train, just in case Revelle had missed the early morning departure but her daughter was not on that one either. Jan Balmain sensed something was horribly wrong almost straight away. She went home and phoned every hospital in Sydney – nothing. That evening Jan phoned the police and reported her daughter missing.

She didn't know at the time but someone else had already lodged a missing persons report about Revelle, almost 24 hours earlier. Piers Fisher-Pollard, Revelle's boyfriend, had called police the night before to tell them he couldn't find her. They told him not to worry too much, his girlfriend had probably just gone walkabout.

Although they were slow to begin the investigation, one of the first things police discovered about Revelle was that she had a secret: she had been working as a high-class escort. That revelation may have influenced their lack of urgency in opening the case. They didn't commence enquiries into her disappearance until Monday, 7 November – fully 38 hours after Revelle had last been heard from.

***

Saturday, 6 November 1994, started out as a great day for Revelle Balmain. She was with her boyfriend, Piers, a man she had only met about six weeks previously, but who she felt really optimistic about building a future with. She had confided to friends that she was already falling in love with him. They'd met in a nightclub through a mutual friend, had their first date a week later, and it went from there. Piers knew she was leaving for Japan – they'd talked about it and decided there would be a future for them when she came home. Piers, who was 27 at the time, worked in the film industry. He had no idea she was working as an escort, he only knew she was an upbeat and generous girl from a good family, who worked hard, and had just got her big break in the modelling world.

Late that morning Piers developed a headache. He told her he needed to lie down, so at lunchtime he drove Revelle to a bus stop. She was going to visit friends in Paddington and the couple made plans to catch up later that evening.

Only Revelle knew that she had appointment that afternoon – with a client. The booking was for 4 p.m. in the suburb of Kingsford, and Revelle, in her escort persona as 'Mischa', arrived on time. She dressed in a calf-length green skirt and cream button-up cardigan. Around her neck she wore a cobalt-blue glass necklace. Her client was a young man from an affluent Sydney family, Gavin Owen Samer.

A little over three hours later, at 7.15 p.m., Revelle called her friend Kate Brentnell, and said her appointment was over. She said she was heading over to her boyfriend's place but organised to catch up with Kate for a drink at the Royal Hotel in Paddington beforehand. Was that call made from Samer's house, from the Red Tomato Inn – the hotel Samer said he had dropped Revelle off at when their appointment had finished – or somewhere else? It didn't appear that Revelle had any sense of being in danger when she called Kate. It was the last time anyone is known to have heard from Revelle Balmain – other than the person responsible for her disappearance.

Police knocked on the door of Gavin Samer's house in McNair Avenue, Kingsford, on Monday. He invited them in, and seemed willing to talk. He freely admitted to having engaged Revelle's services two days previously. He told police she had arrived on time, had stayed around three hours and at 7 p.m. he had driven her to the Red Tomato Inn in Kingsford and then gone back home. He explained that he spent a quiet evening at home watching television and had then gone to bed.

Police noticed Samer had scratches on his hands, neck and face. They asked him where they came from and he explained them away. He told them that he'd been surfing and had an accident.

Police looked around the house and found nothing unusual; there was no sign of Revelle, or any of her belongings. They did notice that the house had been cleaned and the wheelie bin had been emptied by the council, but their search was cursory. As there was no evidence of a crime having been committed, and no body, they saw no justification for a forensic examination of the house.

Police went to the Red Tomato Inn, an old corner hotel in a busy part of Kingsford, and spoke to people who had been there that Saturday night. Nobody recalled having seen Revelle there, or even being dropped off in front of the hotel.

Police also questioned Piers Fisher-Pollard. They knew that most homicides are committed by someone close to the victim, and he was Revelle's boyfriend. Maybe he hadn't liked her working as an escort, become jealous and done something to her. However, when they interviewed Fisher-Pollard, it quickly became apparent that he didn't know about her secret escort work, and his distress over her disappearance seemed real. He also offered to provide a sample of his DNA before the police even thought to ask him for it. Fisher-Pollard was quickly eliminated as a suspect.

Detectives went to see the frantic Jan Balmain the same Monday their colleagues knocked on Samer's door. They told Jan that they had found some of Revelle's belongings: a cork platform shoe, makeup bag, diary and the keys to her Bellevue Hill unit. They had been found scattered over four separate streets in Kingsford, as if someone had been driving through the neighbourhood and randomly thrown things out the window of a car.

A detective also asked Jan if she knew her daughter had been working as a high-class escort. Jan was stunned.

It didn't take Jan and her family long to spring into action. Revelle's sister, Suellen, drove up from her home in Melbourne as soon as she heard the news. The family created Missing Person posters and stuck them up everywhere they could think of. Suellen contacted the police for updates. Was there any news? Had they discovered new leads? Could they give the family any information? Jan mustered her courage and went to visit the escort agency Select Companions; she was furious, she wanted answers. The agency was unhelpful and told her to leave. Later they got their solicitor to write to Jan, instructing her that she needed to stay away and leave them alone or there would be consequences.

Jan, refusing to accept no for an answer, found Revelle's telephone contacts and got in touch with other workers. She wanted information, a lead, a snippet of this part of her daughter's life that had been such a mystery to her. Of everything she learned, one thing broke her heart. Gavin Samer was going to be Revelle's last client. She had intended to do this job, trying to accumulate extra money for her trip to Japan, and then she had been leaving escort work forever.

***

Escort agencies differ from brothels in that they are mostly a booking and recruitment agency. They organise anything from a one-hour service through to a lengthy vacation or boat cruise, in which a customer can have a woman as their companion – as long as they can afford to pay for her. They try and set their own standards for the kind of women and men they recruit; their understanding of the practical workings of the industry means they know that the more beautiful, exotic or unattainable the escort looks, the more they can usually charge the client. And of course the agency takes its percentage.

Revelle had actually been working for two different agencies. The main one was Select Companions, run by Jane and Zoran Stanojevic. She was also on the books at VIP Hostesses and worked occasionally for them.

During police investigations into her disappearance, police looked closely at Zoran Stanojevic. They had received tips that Stanojevic was angry with Revelle for moonlighting with the other escort agency. He had given police conflicting accounts of his whereabouts on the day of Revelle's disappearance, yet maintained he had nothing to do with it.

On the evening Revelle went missing, Stanojevic was chauffeuring escorts to and from appointments. He told police he hadn't seen Revelle, that he had been driving another escort – whose working name was Kerry – to and from three other jobs. According to Stanojevic, Revelle had been booked for one of those appointments later on the Saturday night, and the agency had needed to scramble in order to find a replacement when Revelle refused to answer her pager. It was an intriguing snippet of information for investigators who were trying to fit pieces into an increasingly odd-looking puzzle. What time was Revelle's late-night booking? When did Stanojevic realise she was not going to make it?

The information didn't gel with what police were to learn from Revelle's friends. At 7.15 p.m. that Saturday night she was on her way to meet Kate Brentnell for drinks in Paddington. Then she was going to meet her boyfriend. She had also told colleagues that Samer was to be her last ever client. It begged the question: was Stanojevic telling the truth? Did Revelle Balmain really have another agency appointment that night? If she did, when did Stanojevic become aware she wasn't going to show up? And who had been her driver to her agency bookings?

Despite an intensive search by her family, which included widespread appeals through the media, there was no sign of the missing young woman. The New South Wales government offered a reward of $100 000 for information that would solve her mysterious disappearance. The family conducted their own searches. Her sister Suellen was relentless; she walked endless dirt tracks, bushland and beaches in her efforts to find her sister. She campaigned in the media, trying to keep Revelle's investigation fresh in the eyes of the police. The head of the investigation got so annoyed with her that he finally told her she needed counselling. Jan and Ivor had long ago accepted that their beloved daughter was dead, but Suellen held on to a glimmer of hope – Revelle was out there somewhere, she just needed to find her.

Gavin Samer and Zoran Stanojevic, the two people of most interest to police in the investigation, maintained their positions.

Both said they had nothing to do with it, that they knew absolutely nothing about the disappearance of Revelle Balmain.

Years went by, and then in 1999 an inquest was held. Numerous witnesses were called, and witness statements from others were presented in court. Jane Stanojevic, co-manager of Select Companions, gave evidence. Revelle was fussy, she said. When she had signed on with the agency she had told them her conditions: no oldies, no uglies and no ethnics. She reiterated that Revelle had been unreliable, even more so than most of the escorts on their books.

Various clients proffered witness statements. Most of them were less than illuminating, merely saying she had been an escort, a call girl. One described her as 'a nasty little gold digger with a bad coke habit'.[36] If Revelle had a cocaine habit, it was discreet. Very few people mentioned it, and her boyfriend was surprised to hear the allegation.

Michelle Oswald-Sealy had been Gavin Samer's girlfriend at the time. She told the inquest that she had been shocked when he confessed he had hired an escort, and angry that he admitted to her that he had pawned her clarinet for $400 to pay for the escort's services. Michelle also claimed that there were a lot of discrepancies between the story he told her about that day, and the one he offered to police. She described Samer as a 'bit of a know-it-all' and recounted that in one conversation he had told her the police would never find Revelle – that a body could easily be hidden where it would never be found.

Michelle also told the inquest she had been surprised that her boyfriend had cleaned the house. She had noticed the sheets had been washed, as well as his clothes.

In the end, the inquest found very little that was revealing, or that would help police or Revelle's family. The coroner agreed with her family, that the police investigation had not been thorough, and that the investigation could have been handled much better.

The then Deputy State Coroner Joh Abernethy presided over the enquiry. He returned an open finding but said that Revelle had most likely met with foul play. Although he named Gavin Samer as the most likely person to have been involved in Revelle's disappearance, he said there was not enough evidence to proceed with charges against the Kingsford man.

Another eight years went by, then in 2007, then Premier of New South Wales Kristina Keneally announced the formation of Strikeforce Aramac whose job it would be to open an investigation into Revelle Balmain's cold case. Premier Keneally also announced that the government was increasing the reward money from $100 000 to $250 000.

By this time Gavin Samer had left the house in Kingsford and gone overseas. Nobody seemed to know where he was, but his friends told police they thought he was somewhere in Israel.

In 2008, police went back to Samer's old house in Kingsford, and this time they took members of the forensic team with them. Commander of the Homicide Squad, Detective Superintendent Geoff Beresford said the cold case unit, using advances in forensic procedures, had gathered new evidence. It was highly suggestive that Revelle had been killed in that house.

Also in that year, police launched a search for Gavin Samer who appeared to have fallen off the grid. They received a tip – he was in Cygnet, in Tasmania. It was a strange place to hide; a small community where everyone knows everyone, a tiny hamlet in the heart of the fertile Huon Valley and home to less than 1000 people. It is a mecca for artists and musicians and people seeking an alternate lifestyle. And Samer was there.

New South Wales detectives flew down to Hobart in 2008, and arranged to drive the 55 kilometres that would take them south of the capital to Cygnet. Detectives prepared to meet with Samer. They wanted to interview him and to try and obtain a sample of his DNA. Was it for exclusionary purposes? Did they have evidence against which to compare it? Whatever the outcome of their investigation, Gavin Samer remains their prime suspect. And he is still a free man.

**

A few years after Revelle went missing, Ivor and Jan Balmain moved to Queensland. The memories of their daughter's disappearance and their futile attempts to find her were overwhelming. Life had become too painful so they decided to pack up and start afresh. Tragically, Ivor died in 2011, without ever learning what had happened to his beloved daughter. It had been a terrible loss when their son, Matthew, had drowned when he was an infant. It had devastated Ivor when his daughter vanished 18 years later.

Revelle Balmain has now been missing for more years than she lived, and the yearning to know what happened, to find out where she is and say goodbye, is as strong as ever in the hearts of her mother and sister.

Somebody knows the secret, knows that with one phone call they could end the relentless torture that has shadowed this family since her disappearance. But they won't, most likely because they don't want to be caught and face the consequences of what they did. Because they won't say, their ongoing silence ensures there will always be more than one victim of this terrible crime – the family, whose nightmares may never go away.

Forgotten Victims
DONNA HICKS
21 April 1995

Donna Anne Hicks loved life. She liked to party. She was the kind of woman who was always up for a laugh, ready with a quick smile for a good time. She was also a mother-of-three, a daughter, a friend.

Publicly her life has been reduced to a by-line in the footnotes of her killer, who is now notorious and a household name across Australia. To the man who killed her, she was just another prostitute, an easy target. Nothing more than prey to feed his predatory ways. To the press, her life meant nothing compared to the more high profile victims of her killer. But to those who knew her, who loved her, she was everything. Her mother Barbara has to live with knowing that she outlived her own daughter, the nightmare of any parent. Her children have to reach their milestones in life without a mother to call for congratulations or condolences.

Donna had never had much luck, not in life and not in her relationships. Men drifted in and out of her life but the one thing that remained, the one constant, was her drug habit. Street prostitution was her regular way of feeding that habit.

Donna's lifestyle – the relationships, drugs and other problems –

were not, she decided, a suitable environment for her children. A loving mother, despite everything else, she allowed her children, then aged nine, six and five, to live with her mother, Barbara.

But Donna loved her children, they were still her children regardless of living arrangements, and she was a very regular visitor and often arrived in the mornings to take them to school. She was still very much involved in their lives and dreamed of the day when her problems could be solved and her babies could live with her again, full time.

The last time her children saw her alive was just two days before her murder. Donna arrived at their door with a puppy in her arms. A gift for her children. The dog that they'd wished and begged for. It was a happy time for the whole family as the puppy licked and played and the children giggled and patted the dog, and hugged their mum joyfully.

Two days later, on Friday, 21 April 1995, Donna decided it was party time. At about 10 p.m. she arrived at the Colyton Hotel, a pub she frequented, in western Sydney. Patrons said she was almost impossible to miss in her very tight and very short dress, her pink thongs, and black dog collar around her neck.

As the night wore on Donna became even harder to miss. She became increasingly drunk and with it, loud and boisterous. She became so disruptive, in fact, that just after midnight the security staff at the hotel ordered her to leave.

Donna didn't argue or cause a scene; she simply picked up her two beers, one in each hand, and headed outside. Ronald Zanker, a man she'd met that night, followed her out, and the two sat outside the pub for some time drinking the beers and smoking cigarettes.

Zanker asked Donna to come back to his house for sex, but she refused. Instead, she said, she was heading to her regular patch outside of the Minchinbury fruit and vegetable market on the Great Western Highway, to meet up with her pimp and maybe earn a few dollars before calling it a night.

Zanker still thought he was in with a chance. He walked with her from the pub to the market with Donna fondling him sexually on the way.

That had to be a good sign that he could still take Donna back to his place later, he reasoned, so he decided to wait. Zanker sat on a grassy area outside the market and watched Donna walk towards the highway where she stood for a short time with her thumb out for a ride.

Donna wasn't waiting long before Zanker saw a distinctive four-wheel-drive ute with a black canopy pull up alongside her. She had a short chat through the car window with the driver, presumably outlining fees and securing the transaction, before she smiled broadly at Zanker, waved, and told him she'd be back in half an hour.

Donna got into the car and Zanker watched it drive away into the night. He wouldn't see Donna, though he waited, in half an hour, or ever again.

Donna was clearly inebriated, but she was a happy drunk, particularly happy now that she'd found a client so quickly. Perhaps she thought Ron would still be waiting when she got back. They could finish the party. A few more drinks wouldn't hurt and it might be a nice change of pace to actually wake up in a man's arms. Ron seemed like a pretty decent bloke, why not?

Donna talked happily to the man beside her, laughing loudly at her own jokes. She didn't seem to notice that he barely responded, staring straight ahead into the darkness.

They pulled into a deserted car park near a quarry in suburban Sydney. Donna was told to get out of the car, which she did, and she stood waiting. He ordered her to strip. This was unusual for Donna; usually her clients were in a hurry to get it over and done with, barely bothering with removing clothes, other than what was absolutely necessary to get the job done. Standing in the darkness, in that isolated place must have sobered Donna up a little and her internal alarm bells may have started ringing. She hesitated and tried to renegotiate with the man, suggesting they go somewhere else, maybe some place more comfortable – a hotel or even her place.

He would have none of it and told her again to take off her clothes. Donna was scared now but perhaps she thought if she could just get him done quickly, she could get home where she'd be safe and warm.

The man grabbed her and pushed her roughly down, forcing her to have both vaginal and anal sex without protection. Finally he was finished with her and a sobbing Donna thought her ordeal was over. But then she felt the cold steel of a gun pressed to the back of her head, pushing her face against the hard ground.

Donna begged for her life, begged to be able to see her babies' sweet, smiling faces again. Her pleas were silenced with a single shot. Her lifeless body was rolled unceremoniously into a ditch and the man disappeared into the night.

Donna's body, naked save for the dog collar around her neck, was discovered the next day in a drainage ditch near the entrance to the quarry. An investigation ensued, DNA samples were taken, but no suspects were found.

KRISTY HARTY
17 June 1997

Kristy Harty was a sweet-natured girl, by all accounts. When Kristy was young she sat an IQ test. The results showed a slightly lower than average intelligence, not quite at the level of special needs but an indication that she might struggle with maths or English skills, or her ability to judge a situation. It certainly didn't impede her ability to make friends, to be a caring person or to be remembered fondly.

She was the apple of her father's eye. In 1989, when Kristy was just 10 years old, her world collapsed. Kristy's father was tragically killed in an accident and Kristy was unable to find a way to cope with her grief – or understand it. That grief consumed her and she began to head down a very troubled path.

The usual support networks were not available to Kristy. Her mother was admitted to psychiatric care so Kristy and her younger brother were left without either parent to guide them. The two were placed in the care of their grandfather. An elderly gentleman with health issues of his own, the grandfather was unequipped to deal with two small children, let alone two who had experienced such extreme trauma. Added to that were Kristy's own learning difficulties and those of her brother, who attended a special school for his severe special needs.

It was a recipe for disaster.

Kristy and her brother were regularly taken from their grandfather and placed in the care of foster families. Most often they were separated; finding a suitable placement for two such high-need children was near impossible. The one link Kristy had to her former life, her only constant, was severed.

Life in foster care was a life of uncertainty. One teacher

from Naranga, the special school that Kristy's brother attended, recalls with much anguish and heartbreak the small boy arriving to school each day dragging a black rubbish bag behind him. The contents of that bag were everything he owned – his whole life reduced to one plastic garbage bag. She said he did so because he never knew where he would be at the end of the school day. Never knew who would be picking him up or where they would take him.

Kristy was shipped around from one family to another and from one state-run halfway house to another, never sure of what tomorrow would bring. Whilst in care, on more than one occasion, Kristy was abused, physically, emotionally and sexually. She soon learned that everything you care about can be taken away in an instant, that life is cheap – some people's cheaper than others – and that her body was a commodity. Others would use it anyway, she figured, so she should have the right to choose by whom and for how much.

By the age of 15, Kristy had turned to drugs, particularly the highly addictive heroin. If she couldn't cope with the grief, couldn't cope with the roller coaster that her life had become, then, she reasoned, she could just wipe it out. Just stop feeling. Heroin became her best friend, her only constant in a world of uncertainty. Other friends dropped away, as did what remained of her family, unable to break through the defensive barriers that Kristy was constructing around herself.

Heroin may have been Kristy's only remaining friend, but it doesn't show any loyalty. And it doesn't come cheap. To sustain her habit, Kristy began work at a brothel. This didn't last long as Kristy's habit made her unreliable. Her only option was to turn tricks amongst acquaintances and drug dealers, trading herself for the drug she needed so badly. Occasionally, when clients weren't forthcoming, or times were particularly bad,

Kristy would turn to the streets, soliciting passing motorists for sex.

In June 1997, not long after she had turned 18, Kristy approached several people, friends and acquaintances, for money. She was in desperate need of $90, she said, to pay off a drug debt. Nobody was able to help her. It's probable that many of them had similar debts of their own to worry about, or that Kristy had borrowed or asked to borrow too many such sums in the past.

Kristy's fear of the dealer she owed the money to grew so large that she became increasingly desperate. With no legitimate means to obtain such a sum (as small as it may seem to many), Kristy took to the Princes Highway and surrounding roadways, near Dandenong in Victoria, attempting to solicit sex for money from passing motorists.

At around noon, a carload of 'tradies' stopped to talk to Kristy. Another car, driven by Geoff Brown, another tradie and friend of the first carload of men, stopped too. Brown recounted later in court, 'She said she needed some money. She offered us sex for money. First of all it was 50 [dollars], then it was two for 90.'[37]

He went on to testify that Kristy appeared to be 'buzzing like she was on drugs' and noted her confused and erratic behaviour. This was highlighted by the fact that while they were still attempting to talk to Kristy, another car pulled up on the opposite side of the road and 'she just bolted across the highway'.

Around two hours later, at about 2 p.m., driving instructor Paul Puissesseau saw Kristy apparently hitchhiking back towards Dandenong. He remembered Kristy's 'provocative' clothing and noted, 'that kid's looking for trouble'.

The last credible sighting of Kristy Harty, other than by her killer, was at 4.30 p.m. when she entered a takeaway food shop. Greasy potato cakes were to be young Kristy's last meal.

At some point after this, approaching dusk in Melbourne's

short winter days, Kristy was offered a lift by another man. A man whose identity wouldn't be known for several years.

Kristy got into the passenger seat of the white ute. The man took little notice as the girl beside him chatted nervously, trying to fill the silence. The man pulled out on the highway, checking his mirrors but ignoring Kristy's small talk and questions regarding their destination. In Kristy's experience, men wanted to talk. Most men felt better about engaging the services of a sex worker if they could create the illusion, at least to themselves, that they knew the girl.

Not so this time. As the man indicated and the car turned into a lonely bush track, her isolation paired with the man's strange silence may have piqued her concerns.

One can imagine that Kristy thought of the dealer breathing down her neck to make good on her debts, and with no other viable avenues for obtaining quick cash, didn't have the luxury of listening to her instincts. Besides, she probably reasoned, what did she know? How many times had she been told she was stupid, worthless, or a strung-out junkie whore? Best to just shut up, go along, and get it over with.

The man continued to drive down the isolated bush track before pulling over between some trees, presumably for some privacy for the sex act he was paying Kristy to perform.

There wasn't another soul in sight, their only company the trees and the birds residing within them. A few hours earlier and maybe they would have been joined by the odd jogger or dog walker, but not now, not at dusk on a cold winter's evening. And yet, the rush of cars travelling on busy Upper Beaconsfield Road could still be heard. It was an odd parallel: to be so close to so many people, and yet so very isolated.

Kristy and the man got out of the ute and Kristy asked exactly what the man wanted, running through a list of services she was willing to perform, and the prices attached to each. The man indicated that he wanted sex and Kristy agreed.

Kristy had been diagnosed with hepatitis a short time beforehand, and wanting to be sensible and responsible, produced a safe sex pack. From it she withdrew a condom, opened it and began to unroll it for use on the man who stood before her. He would have none of it. It's unknown whether the man violently demanded she have sex without the use of the condom, or if, vulnerable and confused, Kristy was persuaded without force.

Either way, the man had sex with Kristy, leaving traces of his semen in both her vagina and her anus, as in Donna Hicks' case. Still naked from the waist down, her underwear around her ankles, Kristy's face was pushed into the ground and a gun pressed against her head. She was expendable now. The girl who had dealt with so much and had just turned 18 had served her purpose and was now disposable.

Kristy's final moments must have been terrifying and bewildering. What had she done to anger this man? To deserve this? She'd been complicit in his requests and she'd demanded nothing of him. She hadn't quarrelled or tried to cheat him. And yet here she was lying face down in the dirt, semi-naked, with a gun barrel at the back of her head. It was dark and she was all alone. There was nothing she could do.

The man fired his weapon, a .357 Magnum calibre revolver, and ended Kristy's too-short life. He dragged her body to some nearby bushes, barely bothering to conceal her, and calmly drove away.

The following day, two people walking along a bush track near the Beaconsfield-Emerald Road spotted a blood trail. Concerned, they contacted police who soon discovered Kristy's lifeless body dumped in the bush. Again, an investigation ensued and DNA samples were taken but to no avail.

Had this man continued on this path, 'only' killing prostitutes, he may never have been caught. But this same man, the man who had killed Donna and later killed Kristy, would go on to commit one of the most shocking crimes in Victoria's history, ensuring a police hunt that would never end until he was found and put behind bars: the murders of two on-duty policemen, Gary Silk and Rodney Miller.

To Catch a Killer

In February 2003, Bandali Debs was convicted of the 1998 shooting deaths of police officers Gary Silk and Rodney Miller. The two officers were involved in a stake-out for a task force aimed at apprehending the culprits of a series of armed robberies throughout Melbourne's suburbs. The murders were callous and unprovoked and left the people, and the police force, of Victoria in a state of shock. What kind of evil was this?

Debs was sentenced to life in prison, with no chance of parole, and his DNA entered into the newly established Australia-wide system.

Some two years later, cold-case officers finally had their first solid lead on the killer of Kristy Harty. The DNA samples taken from her body during the investigation into her 1997 murder had a hit on the National Criminal Investigation DNA Database (NCIDD). The DNA found was considered by experts to be 360 billion times more likely to have come from one man than anybody else. That man was convicted cop-killer Bandali Debs.

An investigation ensued, police determined not to leave any stone unturned, and evidence was discovered at Debs' mother's house that directly linked him to the crime. A handgun and ammunition matching the murder weapon were seized. In earlier covert recordings, Debs had been recorded telling his daughter

Joanne, 'There's nothing at Roberts' place, but at my mother's place there's stuff in the ground but they won't find it ... there's a few handguns there as well – they belong to me.' In an earlier conversation with co-convicted police murderer Jason Roberts, Debs instructed the younger man on the best ways to kill a woman, 'If you put the rod in the mouth and blew her brains away, when you put the rod in their mouth and close their mouth there's no noise ... I've seen it. I've done it.'[38]

Kristy Harty's grandmother, Lorraine Harty, was kept appraised of developments every step of the way. Battling emphysema, the woman had clung to life for more than a decade to see her beloved first grandchild's murderer brought to justice.

Lorraine Harty had half of her wish fulfilled in life when Bandali Debs was finally charged with Kristy's murder on 20 June 2005. Unfortunately, she wouldn't see the conclusion of the trial and sentencing.

Bandali Debs pleaded not guilty to Kristy's murder, probably more to be a nuisance than for any real desire to fight the charges. His defence team conceded that Debs had had sex with Kristy Harty before her death but that some unknown perpetrator had happened upon the girl shortly afterwards and it was he that killed her.

The jury didn't accept this theory of events. Kristy hadn't had time, or worse hadn't been bothered, to replace her underwear, and Debs' DNA had still been inside her – the suggestion that some other sadistic killer had just happened to wander down a fairly isolated track and happen upon her just didn't fly. Debs was convicted of the murder of Kristy Harty.

In May 2007, Justice Stephen Kaye sentenced Debs to another life sentence – his third – with no possibility of parole: 'You are already serving two life terms of life imprisonment, without a non-parole period ... although any sentence which I now impose on you will not have any practical effect on your disposition, nevertheless the process of sentencing you for the murder of Kristy Mary Harty is an important one.'

In summing up, Justice Kaye told Debs:

> The age difference between you and her was exacerbated by the fact that Ms Harty was a deeply troubled young woman, a fact which would have been obvious to anyone who had even the most fleeting contact with her on that day … Kristy Harty was totally defenceless. She was alone and isolated on a bush track. The killing took place either at dusk or in the dark. She could not have been more vulnerable or helpless … Your killing of her was utterly cowardly.
>
> The evidence discloses beyond any doubt that this was not a case of a sexual encounter in which, in the heat of the moment, feelings or passions may have led to a spontaneous and irrational act of violence. Rather, and quite to the contrary, this was, most clearly, a callous, craven and senseless murder in cold blood of an entirely innocent, defenceless and vulnerable young woman … You murdered Kristy Harty for no other reason than for the sheer sake of it.[39]

Justice Kaye's final remark before handing down his sentence more than sums up the defendant: 'You are beyond redemption.'

Debs was transported back to prison, and the justice system thought they'd seen the last of one of Australia's most hated men.

That, of course, wasn't to be. One year later, Bandali Debs was charged with a fourth murder – this one predating the three he'd already been convicted of.

Another cold-hit on the DNA database confirmed that Bandali Debs had had sex with Donna Ann Hicks shortly before her murder in 1995. An investigation followed where it was found that the murder weapon was the same as one found in Debs' mother's house and that Bandali Debs had been in that area of Sydney at the time of Donna's death. At the time, Debs owned a dark blue Holden Rodeo utility with four doors and a canopy over the open area of the rear of the ute. This matched the description of the vehicle that witness Ronald Zanker had seen Donna get into the last time she was seen alive.

Debs was charged with the murder of Donna Hicks and was convicted in the Supreme Court on 12 December 2011 – 16 years after her murder.

Although Debs' earlier crimes could not be introduced during the trial, for fear of tainting the minds of the jurors, they could be taken into account during sentencing, leaving no doubt in the mind of Justice Robert Shallcross Hulme that Debs had no prospect of rehabilitation and had forfeited all rights to freedom in the future. He said of Debs' crimes, 'They demonstrate … a complete – I emphasise that word – lack of humanity.'[40]

Of Debs' character, Justice Hulme said, 'Considered in isolation, it is difficult to avoid the conclusion that the murder of Ms Hicks was carried out as an exercise of power or for some thrill or satisfaction derived from the act, or a combination of these factors. When one takes account of the circumstances of the later killing of Ms Harty, that conclusion becomes inescapable.'

Justice Hulme also considered a victim impact statement tendered by Donna's mother, Barbara Hicks, before passing down the fourth life sentence to Bandali Debs, ensuring he would never again play any part in Australian society as a free man.

Justice was served, albeit many years after the fact; years where Kristy Harty's grandmother held onto life, kept going only by her wish to see her granddaughter's murderer pay. Years that Donna Hicks' children became adults without a mother to guide them. But justice *was* served.

GRACE HEATHCOTE
4 July 1995

Grace Madonna Heathcote lived and worked in Cairns, in Far North Queensland. She worked under the alias of 'Jane'. On 4 July 1995, she received a phone call from a woman, who made a booking for a massage and agreed to meet with her in a Cairns motel room. Grace didn't realise that the booking wasn't genuine ... it was part of a plot hatched by another sex worker, Kerri Ross, to whom she allegedly owed money. Ross and her friend Kerry Katherine Lowry came up with a plan to lure Grace to the motel, offer her valium-laced champagne, then when she was drowsy or asleep, steal her keys and go and rob her house.

Things didn't go to plan and a fight broke out. At least that was the story the two women later gave to justify a horrific assault. During the attack, Grace sustained several injuries – 14 rib fractures, fractures of the breast bone and broken Adam's apple, hyoid bone, nose and nasal bone. There were extensive lacerations, bruises and abrasions on parts of her face, cheek, neck, chin, forehead, scalp, ears, neck and chest. The cause of death was a rupture of the heart, and tearing of her liver (part of which was described as pulped) – consistent with the victim having been jumped or stomped on.

After the assault the two women stole Grace's keys and went and robbed her house. When Grace's body was discovered, the women left Cairns and drove to Mt Isa.

In court each woman denied involvement in the assault and murder, and blamed the other one; however, they were both convicted of murder. The women appealed their sentence and the judge found there had been discrepancies in the original trial and ordered a new trial. Information is unavailable about the outcome of the second murder trial.

COLLEEN JEFFERIES
1996

Colleen Leisa Jefferies' badly decomposed body was found in her Brisbane home in 1996, possibly more than a year after her death.

Investigators and the coroner were unable to ascertain the cause of death due to the decomposition of the body but it is widely accepted that she died under suspicious circumstances.

Colleen's name may never have been known if not for a three-year affair with prominent Queensland politician Trevor Perrett.

The circumstances surrounding Colleen's death remain a mystery.

REBECCA BERNAUER
7 June 1997

Rebecca Bernauer had been using heroin since she was 15, but in June 1997, she had been attending Narcotics Anonymous for two months. She was trying and now she was 18, she wanted something better for her life. She still worked the streets. Her spot had been near the corner of William and Forbes Streets in Sydney's Kings Cross. Here, in the doorway to a block of flats next door to a cafe, she was 'Charlie'. Recently she had moved on to another spot, but regulars knew her and described her as lovely and really friendly.

There are two different versions of her last-known sighting, but what appears certain is that on the night of 7 June 1997, Rebecca went out to Kings Cross to work.

Two days later her naked body was discovered in Hayden Lane, Kings Cross. She had been wedged, upside down, behind an abandoned refrigerator. Initially police believed she had died from a heroin overdose ... upside down, naked and with her clothes and handbag missing. But the autopsy revealed she had been raped, strangled and discarded.

In 2000, police decided to conduct DNA testing of clients and workers at a brothel in the laneway where Rebecca's body had been found. They came up with a match, and arrested Uruguayan immigrant Louis Pintos-Chaves for her murder. Pintos-Chaves was a cleaner at the brothel. He spent 18 months in prison before the Director of Public Prosecutions (DPP) dropped the case against him. He was released from prison but immediately arrested and deported to Uruguay, as his visa had expired while he'd been incarcerated.

Rebecca had been the main witness in two previous charges of supplying heroin that had been laid against a New South Wales senior constable. The DPP dropped the charges after Rebecca's death.

MARGARET MAHER
4 October 1997

Some people are born predators. From an early age they display the characteristics of all predators, preying on those weaker than themselves, the vulnerable. Violence is something that comes naturally, as do often cruel and sadistic behaviours. The predator will often prolong the process, drawing out the pain for his own gratification, sometimes practising what appears to an outsider as bizarre, ritualistic mutilations. These rituals are the most important thing to him; nothing else will leave him satisfied.

For the predator, his prey is chosen by the ease with which they can be obtained and by the likelihood of getting away with it, and therefore being able to continue with his work another day. Oftentimes this prey is found in a woman walking home alone after dark, or isolated from the pack in some way. Most accessible to this kind of predator, though, is the street-based sex worker. She can be found on the streets, after dark, alone. She, by her very trade, will leave with an unknown man to a secondary location. And, in many cases, she won't be immediately missed. If at all.

For the predator, she is the perfect victim. Such was the case with Margaret Josephine Maher.

***

Margaret had done life tough. Her childhood was not a happy one, and she'd been a troubled teen, leaving school early and embarking on a transient life of couch-hopping and halfway houses.

Margaret didn't really have friends, and certainly no family that she maintained any contact with. She was a woman all alone in the world, cared for, or so she thought, only by the dealers who supplied her with heroin. They, at least, looked forward to seeing her, if only to take her money. And for Margaret, seeing them afforded her the luxury of escaping life for a brief time whilst under the influence of those drugs.

Margaret used sex work as a means to survive and sometimes fantasised about the day she would be able to give it all up. Somehow, she would reason, a miracle would happen and she'd wake up clean from the drug she was so dependent on, with a roof to call her own over her head, and a real job. But for Margaret, steps to achieve that were always too difficult and fraught with obstacles. There was nobody who cared enough to help her make that happen.

Motorists often saw Margaret on the side of the Hume Highway near Broadmeadows and Somerton in Victoria, scantily dressed and trying to attract the attentions of passing motorists for a 'quick trick' and some hard-earned cash. This was her patch and she was familiar with it.

On the night of 4 October 1997, 40-year-old Margaret grabbed a few things to eat at the Safeway store in Broadmeadows before heading off to the Hume Highway to earn a few dollars. Witnesses saw Margaret leave the Safeway car park at around 12.20 a.m., and others saw her walking along the road, but aside from that, nobody saw her again. There was no one to report Margaret missing when she didn't return that night.

At 1.45 the following afternoon, Ronald and Eva McDonald were out collecting aluminium cans with their children, along Cliffords Road in Somerton. Ronald lifted a cardboard box containing computer parts and was horrified to discover the body of a woman with her pants pulled down and her top cut open, lying on her side in the long grass. The woman had been grossly mutilated.

That woman was Margaret.

An autopsy revealed three possible causes of death: advanced coronary artery disease, the effect of drug toxicity and/or compression of the neck. Considered in the context of other injuries Margaret received though, it is most likely that she was strangled. There were marks indicative of strangulation on Margaret's neck, she had a wound caused by blunt trauma over her right eyebrow, and lacerations to her right arm. In addition, Margaret had been stabbed, either immediately before or after death, through the left wrist with a sharp object.

That was not all. Horrifyingly, Margaret had been further degraded after death. The windcheater and t-shirt she had worn were cut from the neck to the waist, straight down the middle with what appeared to be long, sharp scissors. She had then been mutilated, her left breast being severed completely and placed macabrely in her mouth.

Margaret's killer was not brought to justice for her murder until 2005, some eight years after her death. Her killer, it was discovered, had killed before and was currently serving a life sentence. He was the epitome of the predator: serial killer Peter Dupas.

***

Dupas had always been trouble. He first came to the attention of police in 1968 when he was just a 15-year-old schoolboy attending Waverley High School in the eastern suburb of Melbourne.

Dupas went next door to his neighbour, who was nursing her newborn baby at the time, and asked to borrow a knife so he could help his mother peel potatoes. Seemingly out of nowhere, Dupas grabbed his neighbour and threw her to the floor, attempting to tear at her clothes as if he meant to rape her. She tried to fight off his attack and was stabbed in the face, neck and hands. Just as suddenly as the attack had started it stopped, with Dupas running out the door. He was apprehended shortly afterwards and later placed on an 18-month probation and admitted to the Larundel Psychiatric Hospital for evaluation. After only two weeks, he was released and treated as an outpatient.

The following year, Dupas is believed to have been involved, but has never been charged, with breaking into the mortuary at the Austin Hospital and mutilating the bodies of two elderly women with a pathologist's knife.

In 1974, Dupas was sentenced to nine years' imprisonment, with a minimum term of five years, for the terrifying rape of a young mother. Dupas broke into her home, tied her up with cord and raped her, threatening the life of her baby if she didn't comply.

One police officer who interviewed Dupas at that time, Senior Detective Ian Armstrong, described Dupas as 'weak and compliant' when confronted by authority. 'He stood out. To me the guy was just pure evil … His attacks were all carefully planned and he showed no remorse. We could see where he was going. I remember thinking, "This guy could go all the way."'[41]

Dupas served only his minimum term of five years and two months. After he was released, he struck again, molesting four women in separate attacks over a 10-day period. In 1980, Dupas received another five-year minimum term for three charges of assault with intent to rape, malicious wounding, assault with intent to rob, and indecent assault.

A report in 1980 described Dupas in much the same way the earlier detective had: 'There is little that can be said in Dupas' favour. He remains an extremely disturbed, immature, and dangerous man. His release on parole was a mistake.'[42]

And yet, he kept being let out, each time only serving out the minimum term possible to him. He was released again in 1985 and a month later he raped a 21-year-old woman at knifepoint on a beach at Blairgowrie.

This time Dupas was sentenced to 12 years in prison but only served seven, being released into the community again in 1992.

In 1994, he was arrested again on charges of false imprisonment concerning an incident at Lake Eppalock. Wearing a hood and armed with a knife, Dupas followed a woman into a toilet block and held her at knifepoint. Thankfully the woman's friends arrived on the scene and chased him away. Dupas crashed his car as he tried to leave the scene and was apprehended. A search of his car revealed more knives, duct tape, handcuffs and, chillingly, a shovel and a plastic sheet.

This time Dupas served only two years and nine months of a three year and nine month sentence, before being released, yet again.

Dupas murdered Margaret Maher in October 1997 and anybody could have seen that coming. Even the detective way back in 1974, more than 20 years previously, had predicted that Dupas would graduate to murder. The kit found in Dupas' car following the Lake Eppalock incident certainly indicated that he had the propensity for it, and yet time and again, the legal system and the mental health system let the Australian community down and released this predator into their midst. Margaret would pay for those mistakes with her life.

And she wasn't the only one – at least two other women also lost their lives. On 1 November 1997, 25-year-old Mersina Halvagis was savagely stabbed to death as she prayed at the gravesite of her grandmother, just a month after Margaret's murder. She was attacked from behind.

Psychotherapist Nicole Patterson was murdered in her own home, which doubled as her consulting office, in November 1999. Like Margaret, Nicole's body was horribly mutilated. She was stabbed more than 27 times in the back and chest, and in a strikingly similar fashion to Margaret, both her breasts were removed. They have never been recovered. Dupas carefully planned Nicole's murder, having made an appointment with her under a fake name.

Dupas was arrested and charged with Nicole's murder first, and was convicted and sentenced to life in prison. Whilst he was serving his sentence, the murders of Margaret and Mersina were investigated and linked to Dupas. There was little doubt that he was responsible.

A jury had no problem linking the murders of Nicole and Margaret at Dupas' trial. A review of the Australian Institute of Criminology database of all 3723 homicides in Australia between 1989 and 2000 showed that the cases of Nicole and Margaret were the only ones where it was recorded that the breast had been entirely removed. Added to that, DNA found on a glove only six metres away from Margaret's body belonged to Dupas. He was convicted of her murder and obtained another life sentence. Dupas is also a suspect in several other murders, though not enough evidence has been found to implicate him.

Justice Kaye summarised Dupas' history in sentencing and his reasons to refuse to fix a minimum term:

In view of your appalling criminal history, and in view of the particularly serious nature of the crime for which you have been convicted, it is only appropriate that you be sentenced to life imprisonment. Even if the murder of Nicole Patterson had never occurred, I would have no hesitation in imposing a term of life imprisonment upon you. It is clear, both in the present case and from your previous convictions for rape and like offences, that your offending is connected with a need by you to vindicate a perverted and sadistic hatred of women and a contempt for them and their right to live ... You intentionally killed a harmless, defenceless woman who, like all your other victims, had no prospect of protecting herself against you.[43]

Peter Dupas is currently serving three life sentences and will never again be a free man. Finally. It's a pity that it took so long for justice to prevail and take a monster like him from our streets.

The names of Nicole Patterson, a psychotherapist, and Mersina Halvagis, dutiful granddaughter, are well-known. Their stories were told. Margaret Maher was reduced to a single line in the story of her killer – 'a prostitute working in the Melbourne area'. She has no story. Or at least nobody to tell it.

KAREN-ANN REDMILE
8 February 1998

Karen-Ann Redmile was 29 years old with her whole life ahead of her. She was the oldest of three children and, her mother said, 'She loved her siblings.'[44] She also had a six-year-old daughter who she doted on.

On Sunday, 8 February 1998 at 3.30 a.m., Karen-Ann stood on Harcourt Street, New Farm in Queensland, presumably waiting for a client. She was viciously bashed, mainly to the head, and left unconscious and barely alive. The brutal attack left Karen-Ann with severe head injuries and rendered her unable to walk and talk. She would never recover.

Karen-Ann's mother, Lyn, gained custody of her grand-daughter. 'I take Karen's daughter to see her every other day and it is difficult for her. The person responsible didn't only do this to Karen. He did it to her daughter and to all of us,' Lyn Redmile said in 2003. 'Every time we go to the hospital [Karen-Ann's daughter] asks why they did this to her mum. She asks, "When can we take mummy home?"'[45]

They never did. When Karen-Ann's daughter was just 11 years old, Karen-Ann succumbed to her injuries and died from complications resulting from them.

Police revealed that prior to her attack, Karen-Ann was overheard arguing loudly with an unknown male. However, her killer has never been found.

ELIZABETH HENRY
12 February 1998

Elizabeth Henry was last seen alive at about 11.45 p.m. on Wednesday, 11 February 1998, at an intersection in Queensland's notorious Fortitude Valley. The mother-of-six was soliciting for sex on Brunswick Street before she was seen accepting a lift.

At about 5 a.m. the following morning a jogger stumbled across her battered body lying naked and face down, in a cleared gravel reserve in Samford.

An autopsy revealed that Elizabeth had suffered several blows to the head with an unknown instrument, similar to a hammer, and had a distinctive pattern of circular bruises on her back. An attempt had been made, though unsuccessful, to incinerate her body.

When the autopsy was performed it was discovered that Elizabeth had been four months pregnant with her seventh child when she was killed.

Her murder is still unsolved.

CLARE GARABEDIAN
23 August 1998

Clare Garabedian was a 21-year-old woman from Perth. She supported herself and her drug use by engaging in sex work. In June 1998, Clare went to the police and made a complaint against Martin Coates and Amanda Hoy. Police charged them with deprivation of liberty, threatening and assaulting Clare.

Coates was on parole and knew that if he was found guilty he would have to serve more than 500 days in prison, as well as any custodial sentence associated with the new charges. He hatched a plan, and offered a man $2000 to pose as a client, lure Clare to a motel and give her a heroin 'hotshot' – a lethal overdose.

The man known as X phoned Amanda Hoy after he had given Clare the heroin. It hadn't been enough – Clare was still alive. So Coates, Hoy and another man arrived at the Great Eastern Motor Lodge in Rivervale, and held a pillow over Clare's head while they injected her with a lethal dose of heroin.

Clare's body was discovered by a motel cleaner later that day.

Coates, Hoy and the others all received custodial sentences. Coates appealed his sentence all the way to the High Court, but in the end he was given life in prison with a minimum of 23 years.

TRACY HOLMES
28 August 1998

Tracy Holmes was 24 years old and mother to a three-year-old son. Her friends described her as a happy and positive person. She worked for the Border Escort Agency in Albury. On 28 August 1998, she – in her professional guise of 'Claudia' – accepted a job at the Gateway Hotel in Riley Street, Wangaratta.

The client who booked her services, Graeme Leslie Green, had just been released from Beechworth prison. He met Tracy at the hotel, had sex with her, strangled her, stole her money and moved on to another venue where he spent the evening gambling and drinking.

Tracy's body was discovered later that day.

During Green's trial no motive was proven. It was speculated that Green had been unable to orgasm during sex with Tracy, and became angry. In sentencing Green to 18 years in prison, with a minimum non-parole period of 14 years, Justice Cummins described the killing, and Green's later behaviour as 'particularly callous'.

RACHAEL CAMPBELL
7 November 1998

Rachael Campbell, 29, drove from Lilyfield to Kings Cross with her boyfriend, Neil McMillan. He dropped her off in Forbes Street, then went to find a parking spot. Neil was Rachael's lookout. By the time he got back to Forbes Street, she was gone. Neil assumed she had gone with a client, and settled down to wait for her.

Rachael never came back. Her body was found in the grounds of St Joseph's Catholic Church in Rosebery. She was wrapped in two blankets, and a fitted sheet was nearby. Two used condoms were found near Rachael's body and DNA was obtained. There were four stab wounds to her throat, strangulation marks around her neck, bite marks and signs of rape.

Several years later police obtained a match to the DNA; it belonged to Richard Edward Dorrough, a former navy mechanic now working as a commercial diver in Perth. He was arrested in Perth, then extradited to New South Wales. In court, Dorrough's defence lawyer argued strenuously that Dorrough had consensual sex with Rachael but she was alive when he left her. Despite Dorrough's DNA being found at the scene, the fact that he was living within a few streets of the church, and that he was a likely match for the bite marks on Rachael's body, the jury acquitted Dorrough, and he went free.

In 2014, Richard Dorrough committed suicide. He penned a suicide note in which he confessed to three murders, including that of a Sydney sex worker. Although he didn't name names, his partial confession combined with DNA evidence at the scene make it likely that he was Rachael's killer.

LISA BROWN
10 November 1998

Lisa Jane Brown was a 19-year-old mother from Perth. When news came out that she had gone missing there was a collective shiver. It had only been 19 months since the last victim of the Claremont Serial Killer had been found. Was he back? Had he changed his target from the up-market Claremont precinct to the street girls of Northbridge? No, police assured the community, this was different – she's a prostitute.

Lisa Brown went to work on Monday, 9 November, in Palmerston Street, Northbridge. She was last seen in the early hours of 10 November. Later there would be whispers that Lisa was part of a cluster of missing and murdered sex workers in Perth, who were victims of another repeat offender – a man who is serving time in prison for the attempted murder of another Perth sex worker, and who has been named as the prime suspect in the disappearance of another young woman. Yet police also say Lisa was probably killed by her pimp. Pimp? Lisa didn't have one. The only thing that is certain is that Lisa Brown is gone.

JENNIFER WILBY
16 May 1999

Jennifer Wilby was a 23-year-old mother with a young son. She worked for an escort agency and liked to party. Jennifer was at a nightclub in Perth on 16 May 1999 when she ran into Dennis Bell. She knew Dennis – he had supplied her with drugs in the past. He introduced her to his two friends and, when the nightclub closed at 1 a.m., they all headed back to his place to party. Jennifer had already taken drugs and was under the influence when she asked Dennis to inject her with more. He agreed, as it was obvious she was in no state to do it herself.

The next morning Dennis carried her out to his car, believing she was still asleep. He intended to drop her at the bus stop but it became obvious to him that Jennifer was dead. He panicked, and drove to bushland in Karragullen, 40 kilometres south-east of the city, where he left her body under a tree. On the way back to Perth he discarded her belongings in various locations.

It was three years before bushwalkers stumbled across Jennifer's remains. As soon as he heard about it on the news, Dennis Bell fled to Victoria. He had already been interviewed by police in relation to her disappearance, and it didn't take them long to track him down and have him extradited back to Western Australia. Dennis Bell was found guilty of manslaughter.

ERIN SMITH
28 September 1999

Erin Deborah Smith was a street-based sex worker from the western suburbs of Sydney. The 21-year-old lived in Peakhurst. She was last seen by other workers on Canterbury Road, Bankstown, around midnight on Tuesday, 28 September 1999. Four days later, her body was found by picnickers in the northern car park at the base of Macquarie Pass National Park. Erin had traces of drugs in her bloodstream but police believed she was murdered. Erin had been due to give evidence in an upcoming criminal trial.

REBECCA SCHLOSS
15 October 1999

Rebecca Lee Schloss lived in Melbourne with her family. As a teenager she started using heroin and had become addicted to it by the age of 15. For a while she became estranged from her family, and supported her addiction by working the streets. At the age of 16, she served two months in prison, which forced her to withdraw from heroin. Soon after release, Rebecca overdosed and had to be revived. Although prison had brought her back into contact with her family, she remained on the streets.

Rebecca met 38-year-old loner Francesco Farfalla in 1999. He would sometimes bring her heroin, and let her stay at his house from time to time. In his mind they were having some kind of relationship.

Rebecca was last seen on 15 October 1999, two days before her 18th birthday.

Police investigations led to the arrest of Farfalla. He confessed that he had strangled Rebecca, then dumped her body in an industrial bin at Keilor Park. This led to a police search of the Campbellfield Tip.

In court, Farfalla's defence attorney argued provocation, claiming that Farfalla had been taunted by the victim, who had mocked his impotence. Justice Frank Vincent accepted that the defendant had been provoked and sentenced him to just nine years in prison.

Rebecca Schloss's body has never been found. Her family held a memorial service for her at the Campbellfield Tip.

'BAMBI'
28 December 2000

'Bambi' was a sex worker who worked out of an illegal brothel called the Love Shack in Capalaba West, an outer suburb of Brisbane that is now part of Chandler. The Love Shack had been in operation since the early 1990s.

At 8.47 p.m. on the night of 28 December 2000, a triple-0 call was received from a man who claimed a child had knocked on his door and said she had been raped; she also told him her mother had been shot. When police arrived at The Love Shack they discovered the woman known as Bambi dead on the floor. She had been shot three times with a .22 calibre weapon. Bambi's 12-year-old daughter had been taken from the scene where she had been sexually assaulted. Despite Queensland Police offering a $250 000 reward, the crime remains unsolved.

The Love Shack had a reputation. There had been numerous overdoses on the premises and the owner and her partner claimed a Mr Big of the prostitution industry had been trying to take them over. They claimed that shots had been fired at the brothel and at their car, and that staff were being harassed.

On 19 May 2000, their receptionist Andrea Snowdon was executed. She disappeared when she was driving a sex worker home, and her half-naked body was found nine days later. She had been shot three times in the head. Andrea's murder remains unsolved.

A year after Bambi's murder, sex worker Rhonda Karger told a Brisbane court she was being stalked. She feared for her life because she knew too much about the killings – to the point where she had made a tape recording and left it in a bank vault.

From Paramedic to Predator

Despite what popular culture – movies, television crime dramas and crime fiction books – would have us believe, the elusive serial killer is quite a rare beast.

Every year in Australia somewhere in the vicinity of 250 people are victims of homicide. However, according to a statistical study completed by the Radford University Serial Killer Database, only 72 people who fall under the definition of 'serial killer' have operated in Australia over the entire last century, between the years 1900 and 2010.[46]

Police don't ignore links between crimes when they become apparent, but most are ill-equipped to see the patterns and are more likely to work each case in an isolated capacity. When the victims are street-based sex workers, secretive by nature and often transient, the puzzle can be even more difficult to piece together.

Police also often find themselves reluctant to use the term serial killer for two main reasons: the fear that such an image strikes into the public, which can lead to unnecessary panic; and the worry that police would so focus on finding one perpetrator to cover all similar crimes that they may overlook crucial information which could otherwise lead to the discovery of multiple perpetrators.

So when in 2003 Queensland police announced the establishment of Taskforce Midas, a team dedicated to investigating the link between the murders of several sex workers in Brisbane's Fortitude Valley area, the public knew things were serious.

Was there a serial killer in their midst?

JASMIN CRATHERN
11 August 2002

Jasmin Crathern was a 41-year-old mother of three with a penchant for Lifesaver iceblocks. She was also a heroin addict doing her best to support her habit and survive the world that had thrown her curve ball after curve ball.

Jasmin was one of the luckier ones who worked the Fortitude Valley area in Brisbane – she had a place to call home, as meagre as it was. She lived in one of six flats in a doss-house in East Brisbane, sparsely furnished but with a fridge for her food, some basic items of crockery and a TV to relax in front of when she wasn't working. For only $150 per week it provided all she needed for those hours between going out to work and scoring her next hit.

Jasmin was a well-known face around the Valley. She was smart and street-wise and always well-dressed. The other girls respected her knowledge of the area. She wasn't one to get herself into trouble. She knew how to navigate the streets, knew who to shy away from. She was tough and could look after herself.

On 7 August 2002, Jasmin left her little flat wearing a beige suit consisting of a miniskirt and jacket, a black top and black knee-high boots, with her black handbag slung over her shoulder. Work beckoned and Jasmin hoped she'd continue her run of good luck. The past couple of nights had been busy with well-paying clients.

Jasmin popped into the service station where she was a regular customer for a packet of cigarettes and a Lifesaver iceblock at about 8.30 p.m. The attendant who served her would be the last person, other than her killer, known to have seen Jasmin alive. Security footage showed Jasmin making her purchases and chatting happily before leaving the store.

Sometime later Jasmin approached a distinctive twin-cab ute with white stripes on the sides, a CB aerial, tinted windows and a canopy. The ute had circled the area several times that night before stopping. This wasn't unusual for clients, particularly those for whom soliciting was a first. It could take some time to make the decision to go ahead.

Jasmin spoke briefly to the man behind the wheel, negotiating prices and services, before hopping into the passenger seat beside him. The man pulled off the curb and drove away.

Jasmin directed him to a vacant block but the man became nervous when he saw other people around. She suggested another place and again the twin-cab ute roared to life and off they went.

At yet another vacant lot, Jasmin asserted that she wanted to be paid up-front. She was far too streetwise to perform any services without evidence that the client could and would pay first. He gave her $50 and they climbed into to the back of the ute where she performed oral sex. At some point, Jasmin was bound hand and foot. Whether Jasmin consented to the bondage scenario, or if her attacker did this forcefully, is unknown.

What happened next can only be imagined. The man who had seemed so amiable only moments ago changed into a monster and flew into a fit of rage. He produced a weapon with a long sharp blade and stabbed the terrified woman in a frenzy.

Over and over again he plunged the blade into her back, chest and neck while Jasmin screamed and fought desperately for her life. Finally, with 14 separate stab wounds that measured up to 16 centimetres deep and her throat cut, Jasmin's ordeal was over.

The next morning a truck driver pulled into a vacant lot beside the Hendra Police Station, which was often used as a truck stop. He saw what he at first thought was a pile of rags on the ground but it wasn't. Jasmin Crathern's near-naked body lay in the foetal position not far from where police cars were parked.

The truck driver immediately called for help and police arrived on-scene without delay. Jasmin only had her black top on ... the beige suit and black handbag she'd left home with were nowhere to be seen. She had been bound hand and foot before her death. Even though her body was a mess of stab wounds, indicating a frenzied attack, the lack of blood around her was striking. Jasmin hadn't been killed here. Her murder had occurred elsewhere and her killer had dumped her body in taunting distance of the police.

Jasmin's body was quickly identified with the help of other girls in the area and an investigation was started. The killer had left behind more than just the bloodied remains of his victim, he'd also left tyre tracks in the mud, and some footprints which belonged to a particular brand of boot. The police had their start but they had no idea how far it would take them or if it would take them there fast enough to prevent the killer from striking again.

JULIE McCOLL
26 February 2003

Julie McColl was born in New Zealand in 1960 and was immediately adopted out to a new family. Life was pretty normal for her up until she turned 15, when her world was shattered. Her adopted father, the man who had raised her, the only dad that Julie had ever known, committed suicide.

Julie left home shortly after and tried to navigate her own path through what could be a cruel world. Over the years she mothered four children and fell into one bad crowd after another, and one bad relationship after another. She developed an addiction to heroin.

To support her habit Julie would often work in the sex industry, exchanging sexual services for the money to buy her heroin. At one time she worked as a bondage and discipline mistress, a job she very much enjoyed and dreamed of going back to.

In 1994, Julie answered a magazine advertisement from retired country singer Tom Annas, in Australia, who was desperately seeking his natural daughter who had been adopted out at birth in New Zealand. Julie McColl had found her father.

Annas paid for Julie to fly to Hervey Bay in Australia and the two were reunited. What she found was an amazingly supportive father who would do all he could to help her and keep her safe. He knew of her heroin addiction and helped her to get onto a methadone program to dry out. When he found out how she was supporting that habit he said, 'It was hard at first, then I thought, what the hell, it's the oldest profession in the world.'[47]

Julie, however, soon found herself straying from the path again and living in Brisbane, working regularly in the Fortitude Valley area.

Her de facto husband of five years, Ronnie Krux, was locked up in Arthur Gorrie prison for credit card fraud and stealing, so Julie had to make it as best she could on her own.

But Julie was a fighter, and more than that, a deeply caring, compassionate person who, it seemed, everyone loved. No matter how down on her luck she often found herself, she always found a way to help others.

One man with whom she had a passing acquaintance said 'she was a funny, generous woman' who often gave him a few dollars for food when he was living on the streets, even though she barely knew him at the time.[48]

Julie's daughter, Emma, just 10 years old when she farewelled her mother for the last time to live with her grandmother in New Zealand, adored her mother. 'She was the most loving, caring friend and the best mother that anyone could have. She was always smiling and always there for me and for everyone else.'[49]

Julie's caring nature couldn't have been more apparent than when she was living in a caravan park on the Sunshine Coast in 1997. She was one of a few people who helped to rescue a three-year-old boy from what is deemed one of the worst cases of child abuse in Queensland history. The boy was forced to live in a box inside a cupboard, and was battered for two weeks consecutively by his mother and her boyfriend. When Julie called authorities for help, the little boy was found with a broken leg, more than 100 cigarette burns over his tiny body, and had been forced to drink his own urine. Without Julie's actions, that little boy may well have died.

For the most part, Julie McColl was an everyday woman. She loved her children dearly, liked to do needlework and showed some talent in painting. Walks on the beach were counted as one of her favourite things to do. She loved the TV show *Rove Live* which appealed to her bubbly personality and quirky sense of humour. And she loved music, particularly The Eagles.

Julie dreamed of getting out of street work. She talked often about returning to New Zealand where, she said, she had a basement ready to set up as a legitimate bondage and discipline den. She and fellow worker and friend Kay Gardner talked about going into the business together, charging clients $500 per session for their services.

Julie had made plans to return to Hervey Bay to be with her natural father in March or April of 2002, to once again try the methadone program and get herself clean. The streets frightened Julie. She knew the life she was leading was taking her no place good. Her $400-per-day heroin habit was ruling her life and putting her in danger. Once, she had been abducted in the boot of a car, held and repeatedly raped. A suspect was found but the case was deemed futile and didn't proceed.

Julie had options and she intended to take them, to make the most of out of the rest of her life. First she would get clean, and then she would return to her children and the business she dreamed of establishing.

She would never have that chance.

***

On 25 February 2003, Julie woke up in the arms of her live-in lover, who calls herself 'Jane'. The two admitted that theirs was more a relationship of convenience than a true romance – they were more like sisters. She got ready in the overcrowded flat they shared, chillingly in the same doss-house that Jasmin Crathern had lived in, and talked about what was on TV and who would stay home with Jane's children.

Julie dressed in a blue denim miniskirt and white knitted top. She put her dark sandals on her feet, and threw her Longbeach cigarettes into her handbag. With a kiss goodbye, Julie walked out the front door for work.

It was a slow night, rainy and cold. Very few punters were on the lookout for her services. Julie contemplated calling it a night but knew she couldn't return home empty-handed.

At around midnight, Julie and another girl were picked up by police on suspicion of carrying drugs. Within half an hour Julie was released, alone, while her friend was detained.

Julie wandered off again in search of a client. She must have found somebody because the next sighting of her was surveillance footage of her walking along Adelaide Street, quite some distance from the Fortitude Valley area.

Two hours later, at 2.30 a.m., witnesses saw Julie back at her usual haunt in the Valley.

Sometime in the next hour, a dark-coloured, twin-cab ute with white stripes and a distinctive CB radio aerial pulled up alongside Julie. She tapped on the window, soaked from the rain that had barely taken a break since she'd set out, and the driver indicated for her to hop into the passenger seat.

Julie asked the driver if he'd like some company and he said he would. She told him she could provide oral sex for $25 which appealed to the man. Julie started talking to him about what kinds of things turned him on as they drove towards Deep Water bend, a popular fishing spot.

The man told Julie that he was into bondage and they chatted about that for a while. Friends of Julie say though that 'under no circumstances would she have allowed a client to tie her up'.[50] She was too smart for that.

The ute pulled up in a darkened car park of Deep Water Bend, seemingly deserted and silent save for the constant pattering of the rain.

Whether by force or with her consent, Julie's hands and feet were bound with ropes, tied into knots that are specific to those with knowledge of bondage practices, and she was blindfolded.

Soaking wet, bound and unable to see, she performed oral sex on the man. Now she was vulnerable, alone and completely defenceless, when the man produced a bayonet-style knife.

The attack was brutal and frenzied. Julie screamed. A scream that was heard by two fishermen, David Dixon and Andrew Smith, on a nearby jetty. They thought, at the time, that the sound was made by a loud bird, only realising their mistake the next day. 'It was high-pitched like a woman's scream, like somebody in trouble kind of scream, a pain sort of scream that lasted a good 30 seconds to a minute.'[51]

The assailant continued to stab Julie McColl in the back, neck and chest, despite her pleas and pained screams. Twenty-four times he raised his weapon and plunged it deep into the terrified woman's body before she finally lay still.

The next morning, at around 7.30 a.m., Brisbane City Council parks officer Glen Diskin found what he at first thought was an abandoned mannequin in a car park at the Bald Hills fishing spot near Deep Water Bend. As he came closer, he realised this was no mannequin. The mutilated body of Julie McColl, naked save for one of her sandals, lay at his feet, still bound with ropes.

Police who were called quickly saw the similarities between Julie's death and that of Jasmin Crathern six months earlier. Taskforce Midas was formed to investigate the deaths, along with the murder of Elizabeth Henry in 1998, and the attempted murder of Karen-Ann Redmile only a few days before. All four women were heroin addicts who worked the same street, so combining their investigations seemed like the obvious move.

Investigators from Taskforce Midas could also not discount the chance that other women murdered in the area over the past several years might be connected to the recent killings and had to widen their nets to include them in their inquiries.

In 1986, Lillian Bridget Lorenz's body was found in the Brisbane River with a severe blow to the back of the head.

Cary-Jane Louise Pierce was found dead in 1988 in bushland near the Gateway Bridge in Brisbane's eastern suburbs. Her head had been battered with large rocks and she had a cord around her neck.

Melissa Jane Ryan had been stabbed to death on the Gold Coast in 1993.

And Colleen Leisa Jefferies' body was found, possibly a year after her death, in 1996. The cause of death could not be determined because of the severity of decomposition; however, the circumstances surrounding her death were deemed suspicious.

Taskforce Midas had been handed no easy task. The 30-strong team were faced with a mountain of information, spread across four separate victims and crime scenes. They needed to follow up on every lead but at the same time be wary of jumping to any conclusions, particularly that they may be hunting a serial killer. There was every chance that, despite the apparent similarities, the murders were connected by nothing more than geography and coincidence. Yet another hurdle was the inherent lack of trust in police throughout the Valley. Gleaning information was difficult in such an environment.

Fortitude Valley is only about one kilometre away from Brisbane's thriving city centre but it is the night to Brisbane's day. The seedier side to Brisbane, it is home to sex work, strip clubs, drugs, police corruption, illegal casinos – and murder. One street kid summed it up: 'That's the Valley. People get murdered next door to where you live. People will always get killed. It's the same old place.'[52]

Despite this attitude, people were scared. Girls started working afternoons rather than nights where possible, all terrified that there was a serial killer in their midst on the prowl for his next victim.

Locals dubbed this mysterious perpetrator 'the Schizo' and theories were rife as to his identity. Some had it on good authority that he was an Asian gang member, others that he was a local politician trying to scare the girls off the streets, and still others were 'told by at least three different people' that he was a cop.[53]

However, Taskforce Midas did have some good solid evidence – the killer/s of Jasmin Crathern and Julie McColl had been careless and left behind quite a bit of evidence to be collected and analysed. One detective later joked that Midas had been an appropriate name for the task force as 'everything we touched turned to gold'.[54]

Police enlisted the help of the Metropolitan North Prostitution Unit, which had built up a rapport with the sex workers and were able to penetrate their defences in ways the homicide detectives had struggled. Within days, a breakthrough was made. It looked like another sex worker had had a close call on the night Julie McColl was killed.

Jacinda Horne, a street-based worker in the same area of the Valley as Julie, came forward to tell of a man approaching her only hours before Julie was taken. He had wanted to tie her hands behind her back, bind her feet together and blindfold her. He told her that other girls had let him spank them. Jacinda refused – a decision that may have saved her life.

Jacinda was able to provide a detailed description of the man and his vehicle to police. Her description included accessories that were non-standard including white side stripes, tinted windows, a CB radio aerial and a metallic canopy. This description matched that given by the two fishermen at Deep Water Bend around the time of Julie's murder.

A hunt was on for the vehicle and police were able to find video surveillance showing such a vehicle cruising the streets of the Valley on the night of Julie's murder. By a process of elimination, police tracked down and discounted more than 100 such vehicles. Then, as luck would have it, detectives pulled up in a driveway in Narangba, on the northern outskirts of Brisbane, and found a Triton twin-cab ute with exactly the markings and add-ons described. The vehicle was registered to Beth Margaret Fahey and the Fahey family were immediately put under surveillance.

Beth's husband, Francis Michael Fahey, an ex-paramedic, fit the description given by Jacinda Horne of the man who had approached her. The net was tightening and more and more evidence against Fahey began to fall into place.

Fahey was a 'cleanskin', meaning he'd never been convicted of a violent crime before, which accounted for there being no DNA hit between him and the sample recovered from Jasmin Crathern's black top.

He had, however, been convicted of WorkCover fraud. In 2000, he left the Queensland Ambulance Service, claiming he was stressed and suffering from post-traumatic stress disorder. He subsequently had a heart attack and his family noticed his personality and behaviour changing. He was admitted several times to a psychiatric hospital where it was noted he was prone to violent rages, mood swings and blackouts. He was a depressed insomniac and when sleep eluded him, would go for drives. This was a substantial piece of circumstantial evidence as it accounted for the crimes taking place late at night or in the early hours of the morning.

While Fahey was on sick leave in 2001, he undertook training courses which led to him being charged and convicted of WorkCover fraud for which he was sentenced to 15 months' imprisonment, suspended after four months for two years. He was also ordered to pay back a sum of $80 000 plus $15 000 costs to WorkCover. He spent eight days in jail before being released on parole. He should still have been in prison at the time of Julie McColl's murder.

Further information led police to discover that the footprints found at the scene where Jasmin Crathern's body was found belonged to a specific type of boot – the T-Boot – which was standard issue for paramedics in Queensland. Fahey owned several pairs, one of which was processed with his possessions when he entered the Rockhampton watchhouse for WorkCover fraud.

Detectives found that Fahey often trawled internet bondage sites and a woman with whom he'd had a previous relationship recounted how he had subjected her to rape fantasies and bondage and would be angered if she refused to cooperate.

Almost six months had passed since the murder of Julie McColl and police were concerned that the killer would strike again soon. There had been six months between the murders of Jasmin and Julie so if he stuck to that cycle he could be preparing for another victim.

Evidence around Fahey was mounting but they still didn't have enough to ensure a conviction. Knowing that they only had one shot at it, police were wary of bringing him in too soon. They increased their surveillance, placing a tracking device inside his vehicle to alert them if he returned to his hunting ground in Fortitude Valley.

In April, police were twice able to retrieve cigarette butts thrown from Fahey's window as they followed him in his car. The second butt provided police with a DNA match to the semen found on Jasmin Crathern's black top.

Throughout the investigation, police were able to eliminate

Fahey as a suspect in the attack on Karen-Ann Redmile and in the murder of Elizabeth Henry. But their evidence against him in the Crathern/McColl murders was overwhelming.

On 3 May, police spoke with a friend of Jasmin Crathern, Renee Reeves, who told them of an attack against her prior to her friend's murder. She said a man had picked her up, driven her to Pinkenba and then, after having sex, had turned violent. She escaped from the car and the man attempted to run her down.

Police returned the following day with 12 pictures of different men. Renee picked out one photo of the man who had attacked her. It was Fahey.

The following day, Fahey was taken into custody while search warrants for his rental property in Narangba and for his car, were executed.

While Fahey sat in an interview room, denying any involvement in the murders and offering 'logical' reasons for why he may have been in the Valley area and near the crime scenes, police searched his property and car and found metal clamps that matched those found on the ropes that bound Julie McColl, a video tape showing Fahey tying up a woman in a similar way to which Julie had been bound, and a bayonet. The bayonet was found to be the murder weapon.

Blood from his victims was found on the bayonet and inside his vehicle, and a drop of Jasmin Crathern's blood was found on one of the T-Boots he still owned, boots that identically matched the footprint left beside Jasmin's body.

Finally, as the evidence mounted and Fahey became aware that there was no way he could untangle himself from their web, he broke down and confessed.

'Well, obviously I stabbed them,' he said. 'I don't have much recollection at all … one minute I'm getting a blow job from a tied-up bird and the next thing I'm washing blood off my legs.'[55]

Fahey was charged and convicted of the murders of Jasmin Crathern and Julie McColl.

In sentencing, Fahey's defence contended that the anti-depressants he was taking as a result of his work as a paramedic may have contributed to his behaviour. Barrister Rick Taylor claimed his client had diminished responsibility because he had been 'diagnosed with an adjustment disorder, suffered a heart attack in 1999 and also had problems with his hearing in one ear'.[56] The barrister also added that prior to the murders, Fahey had no previous criminal convictions, was of good character, and had a reliable work history. He was, however, unable to offer any reasonable explanation for his client committing these offences.

Prosecutor Peter Feeney said the murders were brutal and must have been terrifying for the victims. He added, 'Fahey must have derived such pleasure from the first killing that it overwhelmed any qualms about the second.'[57]

The judge presiding over sentencing, Justice White, said it was impossible for the court to speculate on whether Fahey's actions were a result of the 'horrors' he had witnessed as an ambulance officer.

Justice White handed down two life sentences, with a minimum of 25 years to serve before Fahey becomes eligible to apply for parole. However, due to Fahey's failing health, it is unlikely that he will live long enough to walk as a free man again.

Following his arrest, another sex worker, Roz Smith, came forward and identified Fahey as the man who'd also tried to kill her.

In July 2001, Roz was approached on Brunswick Street, Brisbane, for 'the works' and kinky sex. At first Roz was worried that police were following them so she told Fahey to keep driving. He did. He headed to Beerwah State Forest, down a dirt track toward a creek where he said he used to fish. Once in the secluded area, Fahey told her he wanted to tie her up in the back of the ute. She refused and locked herself inside the cab. She found a Stanley knife and put it inside her boot, determined to be able to defend herself.

Luckily, a park ranger arrived on-scene and Smith was able to make her escape. Unfortunately, like with Renee Reeves, the case against Fahey couldn't be made.

The deaths of Jasmin and Julie reignited debate throughout Queensland about the legalities of street-based sex work and the possibility of safe working spaces. Julie McColl's father is a strong advocate, determined that some good should come out of the loss of his daughter.

At this stage no suspects have ever been identified for the deaths of Elizabeth Henry and Karen-Ann Redmile.

MARIA SCOTT
28 February 2003

Maria Scott was 27 at the time she disappeared. Maria had been working the Port Kembla strip in Wollongong, New South Wales, and was considered to be something of a free spirit. She'd called her mother, Josephine Krause, who lived in Griffith, to come up and help her try to get her kids back. Her mother agreed, on condition that Maria get herself off the drugs. Even before her mother arrived and reported Maria Scott missing on 24 March 2003, police were being told stories that Maria had been murdered. There was ongoing street talk about it. For months police had been accused of not caring, not doing enough because she was a sex worker, and because Maria was an Indigenous Australian.

There was a rehabilitation farm in the Southern Highlands, a place Maria used to call her little piece of heaven, that she was known to frequent. It was ironic that several months after she disappeared her badly decomposed body was discovered in bushland on the farm. She had been stabbed twice in the back and three times in the abdomen. The state of decomposition made it impossible to determine whether Maria had suffered any other injuries.

Suspicion fell on Mark Brown, a man who lived in Waratah Lodge on the farm. Maria's blood was found in his cottage on the floor, walls and back step. Brown was known to frequent sex workers and had a history of violence against women. He fled interstate when Maria's body was discovered but returned several months later. Brown drove to a spot not far from the farm and committed suicide. In an inquest the coroner named Mark Brown as the man who had murdered Maria Scott.

DARYLYN UGLE
25 March 2003

Darylyn Meridith Ugle was part of Perth's Nyungah community. She was also a street-based sex worker. Darylyn was 25 years old when she was last seen alive in inner-city Northbridge soliciting for sex. It was March 2003. Near the end of the month her decomposing body was found in a burnt-out tree stump in the Perth hills, near Mundaring Weir. All police would say was that Darylyn had suffered a substantial injury before her body had been dumped.

Later that year another sex worker, who had known Darylyn, accepted an offer of $900 in exchange for sex. While still in the car the client tried to wrap a rope around her neck. She escaped from the vehicle but was chased and subdued and punched savagely in the face in a beating that lasted almost 15 minutes. She managed to escape by crawling through a swamp, and the client was later arrested and charged with attempted murder.

Donald Victor Morey had lured her into his car for sex, even though it was later revealed he was impotent. He was found guilty of attempted murder in 2005 and sentenced to serve 13 years in prison. Moray is considered a suspect in the murder of Darylyn Ugle and the disappearance of another young Perth woman.

Discarded in a Ditch
KELLY HODGE
19 August 2003

In the autumn of 2003, 26-year-old Kelly Hodge made a decision to try and kick her heroin addiction. The previous few years had been tough on her and she had become so desperate to find money to pay for heroin that she ended up working the cold, hard streets. She didn't really like it, knew it was dangerous, and wanted to do something more meaningful with her life. But first she had to get off the drugs. Not for the first time, she went on the methadone program, and appeared to be getting things together.

Methadone is a synthetic form of heroin. It's regulated, the dosage is carefully measured, and it is usually taken under the watchful eye of the pharmacist or nurse who dispenses it. Unlike heroin, it is a slow-release drug, so its effects are more subtle. It's clean, so people don't have to worry what it has been cut with, and it's drinkable liquid – no abscesses, popped veins or infections of the blood.

But heroin is a terrible temptress. It offers a rush that is absent with methadone. A ritual. A strange freedom. When life is sad, tough or overwhelming, it offers an escape from the pain, a terrible relief for a few hours. Kelly went back to using heroin in the winter of 2003. And to working in the sex precinct of Melbourne's St Kilda to pay for the drug. She was still living at home with her grandmother, Anna Miller, in Coburg North.

She cut a small, pathetic figure as she stood on the corner of Grey and Gurner Streets late at night, her pale-blue shoulder bag decorated with handwritten texta markings draped across her chest. Kelly Hodge, a slight woman, would wait for a car to slow then stop, and make a transaction with someone she had never met before. She was aware of the dangers; she had once been stabbed twice in the arm by a client who tried to steal her bag. On that night she had gone to the hospital, got stitched up and went straight back to the streets, back to work.

On the evening of Monday, 18 August 2003, Kelly left home at about 10.30 p.m. and headed for St Kilda. At around midnight she was picked up by a client and had sex with him. They were together for around 45 minutes.

At some time in the early hours of Tuesday, 19 August 2003, Kelly was picked up by another client.

***

When Kelly hadn't returned home from work on Tuesday, her nan became worried. It was out of character for Kelly. Anna Miller knew about the kind of work Kelly did, and she was aware of the dangers for a vulnerable young woman on the streets of St Kilda.

When police were initially informed of Kelly's disappearance they didn't pay much attention. In their eyes, and in their experience, it was not unusual for St Kilda working girls to disappear for days on end – running off with a customer, away on a drug binge or even being held captive by 'customers' for days on end as personal sex slaves. They figured she would turn up.

It hadn't always been like this. Kelly was no runaway, nor was she a discard of the state's foster system. She and her elder sister, Stacey, had been raised by their mother Anita who was separated from Kelly's father. Tragedy struck the family when Kelly was just six years old – her mother died from pneumonia. Kelly and her sister were placed in a foster home. They were there for only six weeks because on Christmas Eve 1982, the sisters were released into the care of their grandmother.

As the children grew up there was no indication of the direction Kelly's life would lead her. By all accounts she was a bright, creative little girl who studied piano, tried ballet, took up singing, excelled in crafts and loved animals. Her relationship with animals was a particular passion for Kelly.

Her childhood, while safe and loving, was tinged with sadness. Friends say she never recovered from the loss of her mother. After Kelly's death her sister Stacey told the media, 'My grandmother has done an outstanding job. She sent us to private schools, bought us lots of toys. Nana has been our best friend. She was not just a grandmother – she was a confidante. But most kids at least have a mum. You feel a little bit different. I think that Kelly, because she was a bit younger, it upset her that she did not have a lot of memories of mum.'[58]

When Kelly was a teenager, a boyfriend introduced her to drugs, initially marijuana, then heroin. As it weaved its spell and promised to take away this young girl's pain, the trap was sprung.

If you haven't experienced opiate relief, it's difficult to understand the degree to which it takes away pain. Pethidine, codeine, morphine and heroin – most of which are available from doctors – offer relief from physical pain. More importantly, in the context of addiction, they take away emotional pain.

Kelly Hodge's pain was the underlying sadness that shadowed her life. It didn't stop her from engaging in a curious life as a child, or from beginning to realise her love for animals, for exploring her creative side. She didn't try heroin for the first time as a way of seeking pain relief. It was offered to her, she was curious; it undoubtedly surprised her when she realised that for the first time in her life there was no pain.

***

On Tuesday, 26 August 2003, a motorist who was driving along Old Sydney Road near Beveridge made a horrific discovery. Lying in a gully off the side of the road was something wrapped in a red blanket.

When police responded to the motorist's call they soon realised that it was a naked woman, wrapped and tied in a black sheet, then in the red blanket and discarded along the side of the road. The scene, except for the body, was devoid of any real clues – it wasn't a crime scene so much as a disposal site. All they knew in those early hours was that a young woman had suffered significant injuries, and had probably been dumped in the gully several days ago.

The young woman was Kelly Hodge.

As police began their investigation the leads were thin. Kelly's clothes, shoulder bag and mobile phone were all missing and there was very little to go on. It took weeks, but finally the police tracked down Kelly's mobile phone, and the man who was using it. He strongly denied any involvement in Kelly's murder and told police he had bought the phone from a 36-year-old bricklayer called Novica Jakimov.

That name was familiar to them. They had received a highly unusual phone call from Jakimov's therapist who, having wrestled with the ethical dilemma of client-patient confidentiality, decided he had to let the police know what he suspected. One of his clients had told him in a therapy session that he had done 'something bad to a girl'. The therapist knew his client had a history of assaulting and robbing sex workers, and had read about Kelly Hodge in the paper.

Almost two months into their investigation, on 10 October 2003, police interviewed Jakimov. They wanted to know why he had been in possession of Kelly's phone. Jakimov told police that he and a friend had picked up Kelly at Crown Casino and gone back to his home in Erinbank Crescent, West Meadows, on a night close to her disappearance. He told police they had all used drugs, both men had consensual sex with Kelly and then they had all gone their separate ways. He explained that she had left her phone behind, and he'd had no way of contacting her – so he sold it.

Although he appeared calm and his story was plausible, Jakimov was the closest thing to a lead that police had. He admitted he had been with Kelly in the week she disappeared, and the mobile phone story was curious. Even more curious was that the other man – the one Jakimov had claimed was with him when he picked Kelly up at the casino – denied any contact with the bricklayer that morning. They decided to pay Jakimov a follow-up visit, but when they went back to West Meadows to re-interview Jakimov, he wasn't there. And his house appeared to be empty.

Subsequent investigations revealed that he had recently renewed his lease. It was odd then, that he wasn't living there ... unless he had something to hide. Police quickly established that Jakimov appeared to have vanished.

Investigators soon figured out the reason for Jakimov's flight. A forensic examination of the house revealed blood in the carpets in one of the bedrooms and the hallway. Further tests indicated the blood was Kelly Hodge's.

It took months but eventually police found Novica Jakimov in Lorne, a Victorian coastal town famous for being at the beginning of the Great Ocean Road. He was working under an assumed name in a fish and chip shop, even though he had always worked in the much better paying bricklaying trade. Under intense questioning he admitted he had been involved in Kelly's death, but claimed she had got really angry because he wouldn't give her heroin and had assaulted him. He was, he told police, only defending himself.

Days later, police searched a self-storage locker in Ballarat. There they found the furniture from Jakimov's house, including a blue couch that had a bloodstain on the back. DNA testing later matched the blood to Kelly Hodge.

Novica Jakimov's behaviour in the weeks following Kelly Hodge's murder could be described as either panicked or as a cold, calculating attempt to hide evidence. Her death had been slow, sustained and brutal. All through his house there was forensic evidence of violence. After the murder he had cleaned the property, and then disappeared. He had disposed of Kelly Hodge's clothes. He had injuries to his hand, and lied to friends about how he had hurt it. He had also begun to apply for a passport using a false name.

Even after he was arrested and charged with Kelly's murder, Novica Jakimov maintained his story that she had assaulted him and he had only been defending himself. Investigators weren't convinced – he was a strong, fit bricklayer while Kelly was 167 centimetres tall and had weighed only 50 kilograms.

Of all the evidence gathered before the trial, it was the autopsy results that mocked Jakimov's self-defence claims the most. When forensic pathologist Dr Burke took the stand at Jakimov's trial, he outlined the horrific injuries to Kelly's body that he had documented during her autopsy, injuries that told the story of a beating that had been slow, brutal and driven by rage. Although cuts on Kelly's hands suggested she had tried to defend herself, her body was covered with lacerations and deep bruises. Her vagina was torn, her face was a mess. Some of her injuries had been inflicted with something shaped like the hollow end of an umbrella, others with a balled fist. If the testimony of the forensic pathologist wasn't enough to sicken the jury, they must have felt unnerved by the testimony of Jakimov's next-door neighbours.

Jakimov's neighbours, Carole and Nelson Ham, were pensioners. On the morning of 19 August 2003, they were awakened at around 7 a.m. by strange noises coming from next door. At Jakimov's trial, Nelson Ham told the court, 'There was initially no noise, just a lot of jumping and thumping and crashing and footsteps running around.'[59]

At one stage he heard a woman say, 'God, stop. No more.'

He remembered that it seemed like an hour. 'It just went on for a really long time.'

Carole Ham agreed: '... loud noises, thumping noises going on.' She heard a woman saying, 'Oh God, no.' She also heard groaning that went on for about an hour.

The Hams initially presumed that Jakimov was having a fight with his ex-wife. They defended their decision to not call the police. On a previous occasion when they had called the police (a situation that involved different people), Carole's life had been threatened.

Carole Ham also testified that she had seen Jakimov a few hours after Kelly is believed to have died. He was standing in his backyard. Ham saw no visible signs of injury to him, despite his later statements that just a few hours earlier he had been fighting for his life.

On 26 May 2005, a jury took only three hours to convict Jakimov of murder. In August 2005, Justice Teague sentenced

Jakimov to 19 years in prison, with a 14-year non-parole period. Twelve months later, Jakimov appealed his sentence before the Supreme Court. The appeal was dismissed.

***

There's a tribal sense of community out on the streets. It's more than the shared experience of addiction that draws them together; it's survival at a level most of contemporary society doesn't know – or understand. Driven to the streets by the collision of life events – addiction, poverty, homelessness, crime, mental illness and domestic violence – they form a family of sorts. Not bonded by blood but by the need to survive.

Kelly Hodge was part of this tribe, at least on the surface. People who endure life on the streets look out for each other, share stories about Ugly Mugs – the customers who are dangerous, nasty or just out to rip them off – and warn each other about bad drugs, violent dealers and dirty cops.

They know that life on the streets is tough. It can be dangerous. And they know better than anyone that society looks down on them, is either scornful of them or completely indifferent to their lives.

Kelly Hodge had only reappeared on the streets about a month before she was killed. A St Kilda local described her as 'sad and withdrawn, a private person who found herself in that scene, but not truly of it'.

During Jakimov's trial, a friend and fellow sex worker tried to describe Kelly to a journalist:

Kelly was naive like me. She thought her first hit would be a one-off. She had sadnesses inside. When she found a drug that took that away, she loved it. It was such a numbing drug, you thought it took you to Eden until it compounded your problems and you wanted more and more to be in a place where nothing hurt you anymore. Kelly used to talk about her nan. How her nan knew she was using and it was breaking her heart, letting her nan down.[60]

In the end it was Kelly's nan, Anna, and her sister Stacey who were left to wonder what might have been. They had known her best, the sweet, sensitive girl who had loved animals, who had grown up with dreams and had wanted to make something of her life.

They knew that Kelly carried a sadness inside her, a yearning for the mother she had been forced to grow up without. They tried all they could to encourage her, to take away the pain, and to help her grow into a healthy young woman.

They knew about her battles to overcome her addiction to heroin. She had entered rehabilitation several times, and each time she seemed to last a little longer than before. She had only been back on the streets, a place she wasn't comfortable with, for a month when she fatefully met Novica Jakimov. She was still searching for something that would take away her pain, and her sadness.

She was still a little lost.

The Slow-Flowing River

PHUANGSRI KROKSAMRANG & SOMJAI INSAMNAN

3 March 2004

It's a popular tourist destination for people travelling through the Northern Territory who want to experience the local wildlife up close via the jumping crocodile tourist attraction. Located just 64 kilometres south-east of Darwin, Spectacular Jumping Crocodile Cruises offers visitors a boat ride along the Adelaide River, during which the guide holds a stick out over the side of the boat and entices an enormous six-metre saltwater crocodile to leap out of the water and snap its jaws around a piece of meat. Tourists gasp with fear and fascination as these almost mythological algae and mud-covered creatures demonstrate their power and indifference just a few metres from the safety of the boat.

Wednesday, 3 March 2004 started out like any other morning for the operator of the crocodile cruises at Corroboree. He went down to the boat and started getting it ready for the tourists who had already begun milling on the bank of the river. As he checked the boat he noticed something floating in the water. It was a scantily clad human body.

At 9.14 a.m. he called the police. He told them he thought

it was a woman who seemed to have her legs tied together. The police's Marine and Fisheries Enforcement Section were dispatched to recover the body, and detectives from the Major Crime Unit were alerted.

When police arrived, they accidentally went to Adelaide River Jumping Crocodile Cruises, which was a further 800 metres up the road. They were stunned when the tour operator told them they hadn't wasted their time – there was a body floating between two boats here too.

The first victim, later identified as Somjai 'Noi' Insamnan, was found wearing a pink tube top and pink underwear. Cable ties encircled her wrists, and a third cable tie was looped between them to bind the wrists together. Red nylon rope joined the cable ties to a car battery. Noi's ankles were also bound by three cable ties. White masking tape was wound around her lower face, her arms were bruised and there was a superficial ragged laceration to the left side of her scalp. Red rope was also wound twice around her neck.

The second victim was an older woman, later identified as Phuangsri 'Poncee' Kroksamrang. She was wearing a black top, red bra and underwear, and a large amount of jewellery. Poncee's injuries appeared more violent than Noi's. Her ankles were bound by cable ties and there was tissue missing from the tips of her little and ring fingers on her left hand. She had deep bruising to the right corner of her mouth, and on both the front and back of her upper chest. Red rope had been wound several times around her neck.

As they began to secure the crime scene, police were baffled. Nothing like this happened in the Northern Territory, and to find not one but two bodies, whose deaths appeared to be homicide, made no sense.

There were clues on the Adelaide River bridge – not much

but enough to suggest that the killer may have pulled up on the bridge and thrown the bound women into the crocodile-infested river. Beads from a necklace were scattered on the road, and there were cable ties, some cut or broken, lying near the beads.

Investigators barely knew where to start. They speculated that whoever had murdered these women had chosen this particular location to dump their bodies because they believed the women would be eaten by the saltwater crocodiles. At any other time of year they may have been right because there is a large population of salties in the Adelaide River. But recent heavy rains and flooding in the river had driven more than half the population away.

Police had no clue to the identity of the dead women, though, and until they learned who they were they had no way of being able to understand the events that had led to this horrific discovery. They could only concentrate on the physical evidence they found at the scene, and wait on the results of the autopsies.

That all changed later the same day when a woman walked into a police station in Darwin to report that two of her friends were missing. Her friends were sex workers, she told police, who worked out of the Palms Motel in Darwin. They had been picked up by a guy in a white van two days earlier – at around 4 p.m. on the Monday afternoon, and they hadn't been home since.

***

Her friends called her Noi. Somjai Insamnan was a 27-year-old woman from Thailand who had come to Australia to marry a western man. She had grown up in the northern Thai village of Lanhin. Like many young Thai women who are born into a life of poverty, she saw Australia as an opportunity to provide for her family, and for the 10-year-old son she left behind. She became involved with an Australian man and moved to his homeland. When the relationship didn't work out, she could only see one way to survive, and that was to turn to sex work.

According to her friends, Noi was careful. She was wary of her customers and rarely left her motel complex. She had a reputation for working hard in order to send as much money back to her family as often as she could.

Phuangsri 'Poncee' Kroksamrang was 58 and also born in Thailand. In the 1970s she had been living in Western Australia with her two children when she met navy man Jay de Marko. They later set up home in Melbourne and opened a restaurant there. Things went well for a while, but when the business fell on hard times, Poncee turned to sex work. She and de Marco moved to Darwin in the early 1990s but separated shortly after arriving. They'd been married for more than a decade. De Marco left the Territory in April 1998 after his wife became romantically involved with a former client, but the pair remained friends right up until her death.

Both women had visas that allowed them to work permanently in Australia. They had both been in the Northern Territory for about 10 years. In that time they had grown close. Noi missed her family in Thailand, and looked up to Poncee as something of a surrogate mother.

On Monday, 1 March 2004, it was hot and humid in Darwin. Poncee and Noi spent the early afternoon playing the pokies at Darwin's Frontier Hotel. Poncee had a booking for later that afternoon, and the request was for two women to be picked up at 4 p.m. Poncee called another worker, Budbue Sriwathada, to see if she would come with her to that afternoon's booking but she didn't answer her phone. So Poncee asked Noi to accompany her. The younger woman, who called Poncee 'mum', agreed.

Back at the Palms Motel, where they had been living since

the end of January, the women got ready. The customer had called to confirm. Poncee, who worked under the aliases of 'Ali' or 'Fiona', donned the long black wig she always wore when she was on the job.

The client was on time. What happened in the 41 hours between when the women were seen leaving the hotel, and when their bodies were discovered in the Adelaide River may never be known. Evidence suggests that consensual sex took place, and it is known they were alive when they were thrown in the river. It is likely the women were thrown over the bridge into the murky river on the Monday night or early hours of Tuesday morning. The injuries sustained by both women, but especially Poncee, led investigators to suspect the women had been beaten.

Police trawled through Poncee's phone records. It was one of many leads they were chasing. One of the last numbers to call her was from a phone belonging to Phu Ngoc Trinh. When they first spoke to Trinh and his friend Ben McLean, enough red flags were raised that they wanted to go back for another chat. And a good look around.

***

In 2004, Ben McLean and Phu Ngoc Trinh, both 19, were best friends. They had met on a school bus four years earlier and become good mates. McLean was a local boy, and Trinh was born in Vietnam, and migrated to Australia with his family; they moved to Marrakai in the Northern Territory when he was 15.

On Sunday, 29 February 2004, Trinh phoned Poncee to make an appointment for her services. He asked for her and another woman and agreed to pick them up from the Palms Motel in Darwin at 4 p.m. He agreed that the price would be $200 for each woman.

The next day, Trinh drove his father's white Toyota van to a store at Berrimah where he made a purchase of red rope, white masking tape and cable ties. After leaving the hardware store he filled the van with petrol.

At 2.46 p.m., Trinh called Poncee to confirm arrangements, and told her when he would be there to pick them up. Trinh picked up Poncee and Noi from the Palms Motel and drove them to his father's farm – where Ben McLean was waiting – in Barr Road, Marrakai. It was an 80-kilometre drive from the motel.

Trinh and McLean had consensual sex with Noi; Trinh also had sex with Poncee. At 10.41 p.m., Trinh used Poncee's credit card at an ATM in Smith Street, Darwin. In three separate transactions he withdrew $1800.

When police searched the Trinh property they found a number of items that belonged to the murdered women. They also discovered that someone had recently burned something in a makeshift fire in the yard. When they sifted through the ashes they discovered burned buttons, pieces of metal from women's shoes and remnants of a long black wig.

The search of the house yielded numerous clues that confirmed for police that Poncee and Noi had recently been on the premises. This included Poncee's prescription medicine, her diabetic kit and Centrelink card, a key that fitted the door to Poncee's motel room, lipsticks and hair combs. They also found used condoms.

While these clues were suggestive, all they really showed was that the murder victims had been in this house. However, the discovery of cable ties, cut cable ties in a rubbish bin, a bundle of rope and two rolls of masking tape began to tell a different story.

When the autopsy results were given to the police, the story became even more horrifying; both victims had been alive when they had been thrown off the Adelaide River bridge. The cause of death, in both cases, was drowning. How could anyone be so cold-blooded they would bind two women up and throw them alive into crocodile-infested waters? And why?

When police went to question Ben McLean and Phu Ngoc Trinh further they were unable to find them. The young men had disappeared. In fact, they had left the Northern Territory and had gone into hiding. It didn't take long for police to track their movements, and a week after the murders, the teenagers were found hiding in a friend's closet in a house in Brisbane. They were extradited back to the Northern Territory.

Initially, the teenagers made full confessions to police. However, it wasn't long before a new story emerged – the real one, they said. Ben McLean claimed the bikie gang the Hells Angels had forced them to kill the women to pay off a drug debt. They later admitted this story was a lie.

Towards the end of their five-week murder trial, yet another story emerged. McLean denied being there at all, and Trinh claimed he had merely watched as an Asian gang had murdered the women. He said they tried to force him to help dispose of them, but he didn't do it.

The jury deliberated for more than 12 hours before returning with a unanimous guilty verdict for both teenagers.

Rex Wild, QC, who prosecuted the case, believed it was a thrill kill. He had no doubt, when he tried the case, that for Trinh at least, the motive was purely the desire to know what it felt like to take a life.

Phu Ngoc Trinh and Ben McLean were sentenced to life imprisonment. In 2006, they appealed the severity of their sentences, but the appeal was denied. Trinh and McLean will be eligible for parole in 2029.

Run For Your Life

SANDRA CAWTHORNE
12 April 2004

Sandy Cawthorne ran as though her life depended on it. She was frightened, desperate on this desolate night to find a hiding place. Her back burned from the bullet that had torn into her torso, her lungs felt the burn of exertion. Her feet pounded the asphalt as she willed her eyes to find a break in the chain-link fence. Or a car to hide behind. But there was nothing, not even a tree on this empty, dead-end street.

Her unborn baby, almost ready to greet the world, filled all the middle spaces in the terrified woman's body, pushing up into her diaphragm, putting more strain on her already ragged breaths. It was dark and deserted but for the running woman and the man who followed, the man who had her in the sights of his gun, and who even in the dark with a moving target, had a lethal aim.

She felt herself grow weak, stumble; more burning, more holes in her. She knew it was almost over. She could feel her body begin to ignore her pleas to survive, could sense that her life was beginning to leave her. In the distance she could hear the steady rumble of traffic moving along the highway, but in this street where someone might save her, the only sounds were the gunshots that split the silence. And the deafening sound of her heartbeat, faster and faster, fighting to live.

She was losing blood, growing weak, struggling to breathe, to focus, to move. Finally Sandy Cawthorne stumbled, then slumped in the middle of the road. It was over. She was dying.

It ended just 150 metres from where it began. Sandy and her unborn child died in the middle of the road. The only witness was the man who had come to kill them.

Local residents heard gunshots, five, six or seven fired close together. However, nobody thought to call the police. At least one person saw a truck, in fact got a good enough look at it to be able to accurately describe it to detectives. But nobody went to see what happened, and nobody picked up the phone to report it.

It was later that night, on Easter Monday, 12 April 2004, that someone driving down Murtha Street, Arndell Park caught the unforgettable sight in their headlights: a lifeless body in the middle of an empty road.

***

Arndell Park is a predominantly industrial suburb, near Blacktown, that lies 35 kilometres from Sydney's CBD. The Great Western Highway runs through it; trucks rumble along day and night as they carry cargo in and out of the city. It's a road with a reputation – throughout the city it is known as an area where a small group of street-based sex workers ply their trade. It's no Kings Cross; there's no glitz, no nightclubs or strip joints. The women who work out there have a reputation for being a little older, harder, more cynical. It's handy to the truck drivers who want a quick, anonymous liaison in a place where the streets are tucked in behind the highway, crammed with factories and warehouses. It's perfect for a discreet tryst because at night the area is desolate. Murtha Street is typical of that – a dead-end street that is crammed with oversized sheds all protected by tall chain-link fences. Few people would ever have a reason to venture down there at night.

On Easter Monday 2004, at the end of a long weekend, 29-year-old Sandy Cawthorne decided she needed to go out to work. Sandy was the mother of two small sons. She was also a heavy heroin user, and it was her addiction to the narcotic that compelled her to go out and earn some money that night. She was trying, she had told her mother. She really wanted to straighten out, to give up the drugs. Sandy understood better than anyone the impact her drug use was having on her family and on her unborn baby. She wanted more for her kids, and for herself. But she wasn't quite there yet.

It's almost too easy for society to pass judgement on Sandy Cawthorne and find her unworthy of compassion ... easy, but callous. The people who knew Sandy didn't see the same woman the media portrayed with their scant reports that invited judgement: heroin addict, sex worker, pregnant. She was much more: a loving mother to two young boys, a beautiful daughter, a loyal friend.

At some point when she was barely an adult, Sandy Cawthorne discovered heroin. She didn't plan to become an addict, never imagined she would spend endless nights standing on a street just to earn money. But heroin is a demanding master whose rewards are yearned for: the initial euphoria, the way it warms a body, slows it down, calms the mind, takes away pain. Not just the physical pain, but the hurt – big and small – of emotional damage, of broken hearts. In return it expects commitment.

Ignore the cravings, the insistent need for more, and punishment is swift – and brutal. Withdrawal is painful, hard to bear: aches, pain, runny nose, nausea, diarrhoea, weeping eyes, anxiety, depression, restlessness and stomach pain all feel relentless. All the while knowing that one fix will take it all away.

Almost worse is the psychological pain. Everything that was being numbed, drugged or forgotten suddenly comes into focus. Feelings that are strange and uncomfortable can be overwhelming. People can say 'stop using' as glibly as they want but the reality of withdrawing from heroin is complex and incredibly difficult to do.

Maintaining a heroin addiction is expensive, and Sandy needed more money than she was able to earn in a conventional job. She knew the risks that came with street work, but where else could an unskilled worker earn between $600 and $1000 in a single day?

Nobody knows the reason Sandy Cawthorne found herself in Murtha Street that night. It is likely that her killer, masquerading as a client, picked her up on the highway and drove around to the more private street a few hundred metres away.

Police attended the scene soon after they received the call. Even though they had to wait for formal identification, attending officers were confident they knew who the victim was. Sandy Cawthorne was known to them.

Investigations produced a few tantalising clues. Residents told police about the shots they had heard and the truck they had seen in the vicinity of Murtha Street, both before and after the shootings and a few days later the police found the vehicle abandoned at a property in Riverstone. Any hope that this might lead to the killer was extinguished when police learned the truck had been reported stolen days before Sandy Cawthorne's murder.

Police divers also searched a nearby creek in the days after her death, but found nothing. When they interviewed Sandy's workmates they gleaned information that might suggest a strong motive if it was true. One of her acquaintances told police that word on the street was that Sandy had stolen a client's wallet that contained $4000; people were saying this was payback. This rumour has never been verified.

Six and a half years after the murder, police released an image of a man they wanted to interview in relation to the murder. The image shows a man in his 40s or early 50s with a tanned complexion and a goatee, yet in spite of it being widely circulated through the media it yielded no meaningful leads for investigators.

In 2014, a decade on from the murder, Sandy's mother, Patricia Roberts, made a heartfelt plea for information. Sandy's sons were now 11 and 14 years old and the family were desperate for justice. To them she was much more than the media-portrayed drug-addicted sex worker. She was their mother, her daughter – and the absence of her in their lives was still painful.

Detective Inspector Con Galea had been in charge of the investigation. He told the media, 'From our exploration of her background, even though the line of work isn't what everybody would do, she was well-considered by other girls who worked in the area. We've never come across anyone who bad-mouthed her, spoken down about her. That's one of the perplexing things about trying to establish a motive. There is nothing clean-cut about why someone would want to kill her.'

He continued, 'We have exhausted all of our inquiries on this case, yet we are certain there are people out there in the community who know the truth.'[61]

Was Sandy Cawthorne pursued down a dark, lonely street by a man who was enraged that she had stolen cash from him? Did someone really hunt down a terrified woman and repeatedly shoot her as she tried to flee for her life? Was more than one person involved? It's an awful image, and it's a terrible way to end a life.

Sandra Cawthorne's murder remains unsolved. Her family

have been left behind to grieve, always hoping someone will come forward and tell police what they know; always hoping for answers that might help them understand something that seems utterly senseless.

Punch-Drunk and Dangerous
GRACE ILARDI
19 July 2004

When is it most obvious that in our society some lives are worth more than others? When we have headlines like this little gem: 'Olympic athlete charged with murdering whore'. And when a sentencing judge who considers that a man's 'behaviour in trying to stop her screaming by strangling her' is 'explicable'.

Or when the accused is an Olympian, a sporting hero to be admired, and the victim is 'just' a sex worker.

***

In 2004, Grace Ilardi was 39 years old and a devoted mother of three children, aged 14, 17 and 20. She was from a close-knit Italian family whom she saw at least once a fortnight. Despite some of her lifestyle choices, her family loved her unconditionally. They hoped, as did Grace, that some of the dreams that she still had, possibly opening her own craft business or completing a beauty course, would come to fruition.

Her brother Frank said that she'd fallen in with the wrong crowd, and gotten into drugs, which led to her occasionally resorting to sex work, but that she was loving and caring. 'She wasn't a perfect person, but no one is, and she may have strayed on the wrong side of the law here and there, but when it all boils down, she was very kind-hearted.'[62]

Who knows, perhaps without that 'wrong crowd' her path may have been very different. Grace had been a champion runner in school. Perhaps the headlines could instead have featured her as the Olympian.

Grace had tried several times to give up heroin, but it held her in its grasp. But this time she really was determined to get clean. Grace was on a methadone program and had started to talk about and make plans for her future.

Nothing could more strikingly reflect the kind of person Grace was, or how determined she'd been to change her life, than the eulogy delivered by her former husband, John Darby: 'My love for Grace was endless. She was a beautiful little person ... she had a magnetic personality. She was a person you just could not hate, irrespective of what she's done. This is a disgusting tragedy.'[63]

Mr Darby told of how he'd seen her the night before her death and of their conversation about her decision to do a beauty course. He continued, 'She was on the mend, I'd like to tell you that. I said if that's what you want to do, I'll pay for the course. She was getting her life in order. She was 39 years old and I would have liked to see her succeed in that, but her life was taken in the tragedy.'

That tragedy came in the form of an 80-plus-kilogram weight-lifter on a drinking bender – angry, aggressive and excessively strong. Strangely, the tragedy the newspapers seemed to focus on was that this Olympic hero's career could be cut short, or that fellow Olympians may have their training interrupted by the news.

***

In the early hours of 17 July 2004, street sex worker 'Joanna' was standing on her usual corner in St Kilda hoping for a client. The monotony of waiting and the bitingly cold Melbourne winter morning were wearing thin.

Finally, at around 6 a.m., a blue Mitsubishi Magna approached, and pulled up next to her. 'The guy pulled over, so I gave him my spiel: "Hi darling, how are you, looking for a good time?"'

The man said that he was, so Joanna climbed into the passenger seat next to him and they drove away. Immediately she was hit with an overwhelming smell of alcohol. 'That was the first indicator that I didn't want to be there,' Joanna said.[64]

Still Joanna asked him what he wanted and gave him the run down on her standard prices – $50 for oral, $80 for sex and $100 for both. The man's only response was to repeat, 'I want sex, I want sex.'

He pulled over and turned on the interior light, affording Joanna a look at his face. He had a huge gash above his right eye and it was swollen, as though he'd been punched. He said his wife had done it because he'd wanted to have sex and she didn't want to 'play'.

Joanna's internal alarm bells had gone from a faint ring to full-scale screaming now and she told him she'd only do oral in the car. The man yelled at her. Frightened, she got out of the car and the man tried to grab her back. Joanna slammed the door on him and walked briskly away.

Unperturbed the man immediately tried to pick up another woman but Joanna told her friend, 'Don't go with him, he's drunk and he's trouble.'

Joanna's decision and the protective instinct she showed her friend may well have saved both their lives.

Later that day, sometime after 6 a.m., Grace Ilardi stood shivering on another street in St Kilda. As cars drove by on the streets that never sleep, Grace probably wished more than anything that she could be home, warm and snug in her bed. Likely she passed the time thinking about the course she'd made up her mind to do, and how pleased her family would be of her when she really made something of herself. They'd been so happy when she got off the heroin and onto the methadone program, she could only imagine their pride when she really cleaned herself up.

But business was business and money was money. One more client and maybe she could call it a night.

A blue Mitsubishi Magna pulled up alongside Grace and she walked over to lean in the car window and talk to its driver. Whether she noticed the gash above the man's eye and the reek of alcohol that emanated from him, we'll never know. Either she didn't notice, or she did and made the judgment call that it didn't matter. His money was as good as anybody else's.

After a short chat about terms and prices, Grace climbed into the passenger seat of the Magna and directed the driver to a laneway in nearby Elwood where they could be afforded some sort of privacy.

Once in the lane the two began to have sexual intercourse in the back seat of the car. Grace put on all of the airs that one in her profession must but this client was taking a really long time. She urged him to hurry up. Time was money, and besides, he was big and he was rough.

The man, dark-skinned and of Fijian appearance, wasn't in any sort of a hurry and let Grace know that he wanted to take his time. Grace grew frustrated. Again she urged him to hurry.

After numerous attempts at speeding things along, Grace had finally had enough. She demanded he stop.

Later in court, the man said, 'I was still taking my time, she was still telling me to hurry up, get on with it, and then she said, "OK, OK, stop, stop, get off me," and I heard a sort of yelling sound and pushing my chest, she's telling me to get off her. I said, "What do you mean, stop?" she said, "That's enough. Stop. Just get off me."'[65]

Grace used her hands and feet in an attempt to push the man off her but at only about 60 kilograms, she was no match for his 85-kilogram bulk. He was big and he was strong – and he refused to get off.

Grace hit him on the face causing the wound above his eye, which he had sustained earlier in the night, to reopen and bleed. Infuriated, he hit her back with a closed fist to the face. She screamed and scratched, fighting to get out from under this man and away.

Still on top of her, he hit her again and leaning in close, he bit her lip. An autopsy later would reveal that she had indeed sustained a 'laceration consistent with a bite mark almost through the full thickness of her lower lip'.[66]

The man punched Grace at least three times in the face but she wouldn't give up the fight. Desperate to get away she continued to scream and kick. At some point during this struggle the rear passenger window of the car was smashed.

In an attempt to stop her from screaming, and so as not to draw unwanted attention to himself, the man wrapped his huge, strong hands around Grace's throat and squeezed for around three or four seconds. To Grace, desperate for breath and terrified for her life, it must have felt like a lifetime.

He released his grip and gasping for air, Grace screamed again, this time more urgently. She was trapped under a madman with no way out. Why couldn't anyone hear her screams? Why did nobody come?

Panicked by her screams, the man once again put his hands around Grace's neck and squeezed, this time for about five or six seconds. In so doing he fractured her hyoid bone and caused extensive bruising to her neck, along with 'haemorrhaging elsewhere which resulted from the act of strangulation'.[67]

Grace lay still, no longer breathing. The man pushed Grace, half-dressed, from his car and into the laneway, surrounded by the broken glass from his car window. His fear of being caught in a compromising position outweighed any concern he may have had for the life of this woman before him.

Before he could drive away, he realised that her body was in the way. He opened his door, got out and moved her body aside so as not to run her over. And he heard a gasp from the woman on the ground. Grace may well have still been fighting to breathe. One minute the man was convinced that he'd killed her and was determined to get away lest he be caught in a compromising position, next he decided, on hearing that one gasp, that 'she would be all right'.

Without calling for help or making any attempt to assist her, the man drove away, leaving Grace Ilardi alone and dying on the hard ground of the quiet Elwood laneway.

At around 7 a.m., nearby residents had heard the screams of a woman coming from an Elwood lane. Concerned, some rushed to the scene to find Grace Ilardi lying, covered in broken glass and blood, unconscious on the ground. An ambulance was called but Grace was pronounced dead on arrival at hospital.

Witnesses were able to provide a description of the offender and his car, however, and pleas from police and from Grace's family were issued nationwide for the man, or anyone who might know him, to come forward.

A description was given of a heavy-set man, with dark skin, possibly of Fijian appearance, who was about 178 centimetres tall, with broad shoulders, short, dark hair, and a cut above one eye. He was said to be driving a blue 1997 TF Mitsubishi Magna sedan which had a broken rear-door window.

By the time the descriptions hit the press, the culprit was already on a flight to Fiji. But that didn't mean he was getting away. Mr Vincent Detenamo, a former vice president of the Nauruan government, and president of the Nauru Olympic Committee and Commonwealth Games Association, recognised the description. It was his nephew, Olympic weightlifter Quincy Detenamo.

As head of the family, Vincent Detenamo contacted his nephew and asked that he meet him in Nauru, advising him of the death of Grace Ilardi. Quincy broke down and cried on the phone to his uncle, who then advised Quincy to return to Melbourne and hand himself in.

Quincy Detenamo did as he was instructed and was duly arrested and charged with Grace's murder on his return to Melbourne. He agreed to plead guilty to a charge of manslaughter, stating that he'd never had any intention of harming Grace and that it was only due to the excessive alcohol he'd consumed, and the thought of being caught with a sex worker making him panic, that he'd hurt her. The prosecutor refused to accept the lesser charge and decided to pursue a murder case to trial.

During the trial, victim impact statements were provided by Grace Ilardi's family which the judge said 'movingly describe the loss of a much loved mother, daughter, sister and sister-in-law. Each ... tried to describe the terrible effects of her sudden and tragic death in such distressing circumstances. They have suffered, and continue to suffer, as they struggle to come to grips with what has happened to them all.'[68]

Indeed, Grace's children had never attended a funeral before that of their mother.

The jury, however, were satisfied with Detenamo's assertions that he'd never intended to physically harm Grace and found him guilty only of the lesser charge of manslaughter, not the murder charge the prosecutor had pushed for.

In sentencing, the judge took into account Detenamo's history. He was born in 1979, only 25 years old at the time he took Grace's life. He left school at the age of 15 effectively illiterate, and immediately devoted himself to the sport of weightlifting. Detenamo was one of three athletes to be counted among the first to represent Nauru, a tiny nation with a population of just 13000, at an Olympic Games, competing in the 1996 Atlanta Games.

In late 2003, he obtained a scholarship to train and teach weightlifting at the Oceania Weightlifting Institute in Fiji. The President of the Oceanic Weightlifting Federation, Paul Coffa, tendered a reference on behalf of Detenamo, describing him as 'responsible, humble, likeable and honest'.

Detenamo's family life was also a consideration in sentencing. He was the middle child in a family of seven. His father died in 2002, leaving Detenamo's mother to care for his younger sisters and brother. He was said to have a strong and positive relationship with her and regarded himself as having some responsibility for her. He supported her financially whilst living in Fiji.

Detenamo also has his own twin children, at the time of the sentencing hearing just five years old, a son and a daughter from his previous relationship with their mother who had died as a result of a motor vehicle accident in 2005. Detenamo was concerned that with him incarcerated the children would have no parent available to them.

In 2003, Detenamo lost his left eye as the result of an injury, which, the court was told, had left a strong psychological impact on him, causing him to believe that others were ridiculing him. Detenamo said he had been trying to protect his head when

Grace Ilardi had struck him, but acknowledged that his response 'may have been excessive'.[69]

Detenamo's previous good character, the mitigating circumstance of alcohol playing its part, and his admission of guilt, display of genuine remorse and willingness to accept responsibility for his actions by giving himself up to police all worked in his favour. The judge sentenced Detenamo to just nine years in prison, with the opportunity to apply for parole after only seven years.

Still, Detenamo didn't believe he'd gotten off lightly enough for taking a woman's life; he appealed the sentence on the grounds that the non-parole period was too high. The appeal was won and it was determined that Detenamo would only have to serve six years in jail before becoming eligible for parole.

Quincy Detenamo has since been released from prison. His coach, Paul Coffa and fellow lifters were 'shocked and devastated' by the case, but have since helped him to put his life back in order. He's now a qualified weightlifting coach working with Nauru's best lifters. Paul Coffa said, 'He paid the penalty and is now going ahead with the rest of his life.'[70]

But who really paid the penalty? Certainly not Quincy Detenamo who now gets to pick up right where he left off, surrounded by family and friends who support him, and pursue his dreams and ambitions.

Grace Ilardi will never fulfil her dreams. Her family must live each day without her. Her children mark all of their major milestones without a mother by their side. There is no parole period for them. No parole period for Grace. For them, the ultimate penalty gets repaid every single day.

MAYUREE KAEWEE
17 November 2004

Thai-born Mayuree Kaewee was 50 years old when she took a booking for services she offered in the personals column of a local newspaper.

She agreed to meet 31-year-old truck driver Craig Anthony Lennox at a Caboolture hotel, in Queensland, on 17 November 2004.

Mayuree checked into the hotel on the 16th and on the morning of the 17th took a taxi to the Commonwealth Bank nearby. She tried to negotiate with the taxi driver for a cheaper fare to take her to Kawana Waters on the Sunshine Coast but the taxi driver refused and left her at the bank.

At about 2 p.m. that afternoon, Mayuree met with Lennox and had sex with him, as they had previously agreed. However, rather than accept the $140 payment, Mayuree asked that Lennox instead drive her to Kawana Waters. He agreed.

The two argued in the car during the drive and Lennox reached across and elbowed Mayuree in the face. He then pulled the car over and, according to his own evidence, punched her hard in the face three or four times.

He then continued driving but again became frustrated and

angry because she kept talking and he didn't understand what she was saying. Lennox pulled the car over once more and the pair got out. Lennox punched her in the face and Mayuree tried to defend herself by swinging her handbag, as if to hit him with it. Lennox punched her several more times and she almost lost consciousness.

Lennox said he then shoved her back into the passenger seat and continued driving but noticed after a couple of minutes that she just stopped breathing.

Lennox drove to his home where he collected a piece of carpet underlay from his garage, two towels, and a plastic bag. He removed a ring and a watch from Mayuree's body before wrapping her head in the towels and securing the plastic bag over them with duct tape. He then rolled Mayuree's body in the underlay, put her in his car and drove to Beerburrum State Forest at Elimbah, north of Brisbane. Here he dumped the woman's body in a ditch and drove away to sell her jewellery and to give away the bank card he'd stolen from her purse.

Mayuree's badly decomposed body was not found for 10 days, by which time it was too late for an autopsy to conclusively ascertain the cause of death.

It's possible that the blows inflicted by Lennox's fists may have caused her to go into cardiac arrest, or for an aneurism to have burst. It's also possible that Mayuree wasn't dead before Lennox decided to dispose of her body and that she was in fact asphyxiated by the towels and plastic bag. Certainly, Lennox was unable to provide a reasonable explanation as to why he placed the bag over her head.

Lennox was tracked down by police, in part due to the bank card he'd given friends which was used for several days after the manager of the hotel Mayuree had stayed at had reported her missing.

Craig Anthony Lennox was convicted of murder in September 2006 and sentenced to life in prison.

LISA MOY
3 April 2005

Lisa Ann Moy's body has never been found and no suspect ever charged but it seems certain to friends, family and police that she was murdered.

Lisa was 48 years old with two adult children, and a close network of friends and family, when she disappeared.

Lisa was last seen alive at a service station in Bankstown, New South Wales. She and a friend, a fellow sex worker in the same area, had a system of looking out for each other which included noting down the licence plates of all clients and staying in touch throughout the night by mobile phone.

That night, however, Lisa's friend had driven away with a client and when she returned Lisa was gone. The friend tried calling throughout that night and into the following day but Lisa never responded.

The next day Lisa was reported missing and with the discovery of personal items near where Lisa worked, police immediately suspected she had met with foul play.

In August 2006, police interviewed a client who is believed to have been with Lisa at about 2 a.m. on the morning she disappeared. A search of bushland nearby revealed items belonging to the missing woman. Police refuse to reveal precisely what was found but the discovery was significant enough for them to assert that this was a murder investigation.

A full-scale search, involving 160 searchers including police, State Emergency Service volunteers, Rural Fire Brigade volunteers, and cadaver dogs, was conducted over a 200-hectare area of thick bush near the HMAS *Albatross* air base.

Lisa Moy remains missing and her case unsolved.

ZANITA GREEN
30 July 2005

Zanita Green, aged 32, was born Annette Margaret Green on 21 October 1973. She lived in Newcastle. As an adult she was estranged from most of her family. Zanita was addicted to heroin and worked as a sex worker to pay for the drugs. She was known to associate with criminals and had a criminal past herself.

Zanita was last seen on 30 July 2005, about five days after she had been released from jail. She was at the Newcastle Clinic where she was in the methadone program. It wasn't until 14 November that her brother Darren reported her missing. He told police that when she had come out of jail she told him she was concerned for her safety. Police investigated her disappearance and believe she has been murdered. Her bank account has not been touched since July 2005.

Police are certain that a number of people know what happened to Zanita. They just won't say.

JO-ANNE BOWEN
August 2006

Jo-Anne Bowen used the name 'Cleo' when she was working. A few days prior to her death she met two men, Dennis Tsokas and Victor Pestana, at the Gateway brothel in Petersham, New South Wales. She was found dead on the floor of Tsokas' office a few days later from a drug overdose. According to both men she had pleaded with them to help her inject cocaine as she was unable to do it herself. The men injected her in the arm, foot and wrist. She immediately showed signs of physical distress and began convulsing. The following day Tsokas found Jo-Anne dead on his office floor, yet took another 24 hours to call the police.

Both Tsokas and Pestana were charged with manslaughter. Tsokas was later found not guilty, and Pestana was sentenced to 15 months' weekend detention.

The Lost Child
LEANNE THOMPSON
7 September 2006

Leanne Thompson's life changed irrevocably when she was 11 years old. Until that time she and her brother, Christopher, lived with their parents in Brisbane. Her father, Damian Rockett, was a detective sergeant with Queensland Police, and he had been married to Leanne's mother, Dianne Thompson, for 20 years. Leanne had been a happy child. A vivacious girl, she loved dancing and playing sport. She played in her school's grand final netball team. She used to say that when she grew up she wanted to be a fashion designer or a hairdresser.

In 2002, Leanne's parents separated after finally accepting that their failing relationship was finished. Dianne Thompson would later say that the entire relationship was abusive, and that her husband even punched her once. This claim led to a police misconduct charge against Rockett, and the issuing of a domestic violence order.

Damian Rockett said it was Dianne who was violent, threatening him with knives. Dianne said she asked him to leave numerous times. He said every time he tried to leave she threatened to commit suicide. They both said the other tried to involve the children in 'taking sides'. Dianne Thompson said that when

Rockett moved out, Leanne told her she hated her father and wanted nothing more to do with him. To this day, Leanne's brother Christopher has no contact with his dad.

From the age of 13, Leanne began to wag school. At first it was classes, then whole days. Soon she was telling her mother she was staying overnight with friends, and over time her absences became even longer.

It was two years after her parents separated that Leanne Thompson's problems first came to the attention of anyone outside the family. She was 13 when she went and talked to a school counsellor and disclosed allegations of physical harm. The counsellor took her seriously and reported this to the then Department of Child Safety. An initial assessment was conducted and it was concluded that Leanne was at risk of further harm.

Leanne made various disclosures, naming certain people and confiding difficulties she had with both parents. Her allegations were serious, and the department felt her increasingly troubling behaviour was consistent with her claims. By September 2004, Leanne told the department she was too scared to go home. She moved in with her paternal grandmother, but left after just a month.

At Christmas time in 2004, Leanne moved back home with her mother where she stayed until March 2005. At the time, Leanne was assisting police with evidence in charges against others relating to drug and sex offences. In her statement she outlined her own involvement in drug use and sex work. At this time Leanne was barely a teenager.

Leanne was admitted to Wynnum Hospital in April 2005 for a self-harming incident. She refused counselling. By mid-June, Leanne was residing with Alex O'Sachy, a convicted drug dealer. On 14 July 2005, the Department of Child Safety contacted Leanne who was verbally abusive to them. She denied any violence by O'Sachy and said she was living with him to 'get off speed'.[71] She also denied being in a sexual relationship with the then 27-year-old man.

On 28 July, a child protection notification was made. It was at this time Leanne's association with the O'Sachy brothers was first formally noted.

***

Alexander George O'Sachy was an angry man, who appeared to dislike himself as much as he did everyone around him. His family were well-off, and even when his parents went through an acrimonious divorce in 1994 they made sure their children were well looked after.

Alex lived in a house with his older brother, Daniel, and Daniel's son. The house in Wishart Road in the southern Brisbane suburb of Wishart was owned by their father, George. Daniel later told investigators that George gave Alex everything he wanted: cars, money, lawyers ... and a place to live. Wishart was an area that had a reputation for drugs and high crime, a part of Brisbane that police were very familiar with.

Alex O'Sachy became well-known to the police too. He was convicted for drug dealing, and was known around the traps as a 'doctor shopper', someone who visits multiple physicians to obtain scripts for otherwise illegal drugs. O'Sachy was also known as someone who attracted trouble – and tragedy.

In July 2005, 27-year-old Alex was hanging out with a group of troubled teenagers. Amongst them was 14-year-old Andrew Anderson who, like Leanne Thompson, was in the care of Child Safety. On the previous evening, witnesses told police that O'Sachy gave Andrew drugs, including amphetamines, and alcohol. Not only did he give the boy drugs, but he showed him how to inject them. On 25 July, O'Sachy went with Andrew to his grandfather's house where Andrew was waiting for his father to pick him up and take him to lunch. When Andrew called to arrange a time, his father asked him to catch a bus. Maybe it was years of feeling that he wasn't important to his dad, maybe it was the drugs, or maybe it was the influence of a man twice his age, but Andrew Anderson called his father back, while holding a loaded gun to his own head. When the phone was answered he said, 'Goodbye Dad,' and shot himself in the head. On the other end of the phone, his father heard a thump. Andrew died instantly.

Four years later during an inquest into Andrew's death, Deputy State Coroner Christine Clements examined O'Sachy's movements on that day. But O'Sachy testified that he had lost his memory about Andrew and the events of the night before his death. He denied supplying drugs or having any involvement with guns. Clements later described O'Sachy as 'completely unhelpful and obstructive' in withholding evidence from the inquest.[72] Nobody ever learned how a 14-year-old child managed to get his hands on a gun.

***

Meanwhile, Leanne refused to return to her parent's care and refused accommodation in a youth shelter. Leanne had not attended school for the past six months. She often squatted with friends and with other people whose lives were as fragmented as hers.

On 2 November 2005, Leanne was interviewed at a youth shelter. She made many disclosures about her parents, prostitution, cannabis use and abuse of antidepressants. She said she wanted to turn her life around, attend TAFE and become a hairdresser.

Four days later, a youth worker took Leanne to hospital. She was suffering the effects of having taken heroin, speed and morphine the night before. Leanne reported that she had become highly distressed the night before after a phone call with her father.

On 19 December 2005, Leanne was placed under a child protection order. She was supposed to live at the Phoenix House youth centre during the week, and spend weekends with her mother. However, she went missing from the youth centre for days at a time, and despite her mother's protests, she spent weekends with friends. Not only did her mother not know where she was, she had no idea who Leanne was with.

In mid-2006, Detective Sergeant Damian Rockett heard that his 15-year-old daughter was residing with the O'Sachy brothers, Alex and Daniel, and that she was 'living with' 28-year-old Alex. Daniel and his 10-year-old son lived upstairs, while Leanne and Alex lived downstairs. This made Rockett uncomfortable; he knew Alex O'Sachy, and was fully aware that he was a convicted drug dealer. He also became aware that his daughter was using heroin and amphetamines – and heard that she was engaging in sex work to pay for the drugs, a claim her mother denied. Rockett tried, without success, to have Leanne removed from O'Sachy's house.

Daniel O'Sachy was an alcoholic and had previously been a drug addict. He was trying to turn his life around, to set a better example and become a decent father. He later told police that Leanne idolised Alex O'Sachy, but he treated her really badly. There were many fights and arguments, and some of those fights were physical. He had reported to Child Safety that on 1 September 2006, he saw Alex hit Leanne on the back of her head and call her a 'fucking whore'. He also told police that Alex had given her amphetamines.

On the morning of 7 September 2006, Daniel O'Sachy attended the Department of Child Safety office at Upper Mt Gravatt with his son, and told the department that Leanne was in a bad way and should be removed from his house.

He and his son returned home but Daniel phoned the police just after 2 p.m. to advise them that Leanne was wandering the streets and had almost been knocked down by a vehicle; he later called back to say she was back home and not to bother coming out. He said he would keep an eye on her. Two anonymous calls were made to the police from the O'Sachy house soon after.

At 3.35 p.m., Daniel's son rang triple-0 to say Alex was hitting Leanne and she was suicidal. Mid-call Daniel interrupted to say, 'Alex was killing Leanne but it's all gone quiet.' Daniel said he wouldn't let anything happen to her.

At 3.39 p.m. another anonymous call went from the house to the police station. Damian Rockett was on duty that afternoon. He sat in the station and listened to the unfolding developments at Wishart Road on the police radio.

At 3.44 p.m. Sergeant Paul Caton and Constable David Courtney arrived at the O'Sachy house. They had been warned that Alex was a known drug user and had possession of weapons, including a long-bladed knife. They located Daniel who told them Leanne was gone, and that he'd last seen her in the toilet downstairs. The police looked in the garage and toilet. Constable Courtney said he also looked in the storage shed, but Leanne was nowhere to be seen.

Walking down to a granny flat, they saw Alex. He was slurring his words, calling Daniel a dog for calling the police, and kept going on and on about $250, which he had just been paid. Police left the house shortly after speaking to Alex and began to search the neighbourhood for Leanne.

At 3.55 p.m. Daniel's son called triple-0 again. This time he said Leanne had cut her wrists. The police received a dispatch to return to the O'Sachy house and investigate a report of the attempted suicide of a young girl.

Daniel was upstairs when he heard Alex say, 'Oh, she has necked herself.' Daniel bolted downstairs and found Leanne hanging from a beam in the storage area. (This was the same area the police constable later said he had searched minutes earlier. When police retraced events of that afternoon they determined that it was likely the constable hadn't seen Leanne hanging there because their view was partly obscured by a cupboard.) Daniel said Alex was just standing there looking at Leanne. Daniel grabbed Leanne around the waist to try and lift her and take the pressure off her neck. At the same time he tried to remove the electrical cord that was wound around Leanne's neck in a complex and unusual noose. He called Alex over to help him.

They lay Leanne down on the floor and started CPR while Daniel called out to his son to call triple-0.

When the ambulance arrived, Leanne still had a heartbeat. She was transferred to Princess Alexandra Hospital and put on life support. But her brain had been without oxygen for too long; Leanne was severely hypoxic and she had gross pulmonary oedema. Her life support was turned off, and Leanne was pronounced deceased at 11.58 p.m.

***

Daniel's son was interviewed by police. He remembered his dad telling child services that they should come and get Leanne. He also recalled his dad mentioning she had taken Xanax.

He saw Leanne in the backyard in the morning. He told police she looked tired and that she was walking funny – weird and swaying. He also told them that later the same day, Alex and Leanne were shouting and swearing at each other. He said Leanne was on the ground and Alex kicked her in the side.

The child told police there were several times he had heard Alex tell Leanne she should kill herself. Daniel also told police that he had heard Alex yell, 'Go and kill yourself,' to Leanne on the afternoon of her death.

Toxicology results showed there were low levels of Xanax in Leanne's bloodstream. No morphine, alcohol or any other illicit drugs were detected. There was ill-defined bruising and abrasions on her skin on the front and right sides of her neck. Although Daniel had stated that Leanne's feet were 'a foot and a half off the ground' when he found her, forensic evidence refuted this.[73] Her feet, it was proven, were touching the ground during the hanging. Dr Burke, senior pathologist at the Victorian Institute of Forensic Medicine, also remarked on the complex and unusual loops of the ligature.

In 2009, Alexander O'Sachy faced a Supreme Court trial charged with aiding the suicide of Leanne Thompson, but the jury failed to reach a verdict.

In February 2012, at the age of 35, O'Sachy was sentenced to two years in prison, suspended after six months, after pleading guilty to unlawful carnal knowledge with 15-year-old Leanne Thompson.

Three months was later added to his sentence for contempt of court when he refused to give evidence at her inquest. When he first appeared in court, O'Sachy said, 'I've given my statement. Nothing else to say. It's a tragic thing that happened.'[74]

He refused to answer several questions and was warned he may be held in contempt of court. O'Sachy consulted with his lawyer, then said, 'I had nothing to do with the death of Leanne Thompson. That's all I've got to say.'

Despite the fact that both Leanne and Alex had previously strongly denied they were involved in a sexual relationship, DNA that was taken from Leanne's body after she died proved they were lying. A witness also claimed that Alex told them it was the ultimate payback to be 'fucking a copper's daughter'.[75]

Numerous witnesses revealed that Alex was a heavy drug user and was abusive and violent towards women, especially those with whom he was in a relationship. The coroner found there was incontrovertible evidence that Alex O'Sachy was abusive and physically violent towards Leanne.

In his summation of the inquest, held in April and May 2013, Brisbane Coroner John Lock included in his closing remarks:

> The person who has likely seen her last is Alex O'Sachy. He has not given any sworn evidence tested through a forensic examination of his evidence. There is no objective forensic evidence Leanne struggled, was seriously assaulted or was defending herself. I accept there was something in the nature of the pushing and punching as described by Daniel and she could have been kicked as described by N [Daniel's 10-year-old son]. The absence of bruising may be explainable by the fact there is no evidence of the force used and the evidence of footwear is equivocal. Not a lot of force may have been used.
>
> The forensic evidence supports a finding that if she has died of hanging she was not fully suspended. The injuries to the neck were not those of a typical hanging case. Dr Burke thought the injuries were consistent with hanging or strangulation and he would consider the cause unascertained. Dr Olumbe and Prof Duflou were more accepting of the case being one of hanging, notwithstanding the odd features.
>
> There is clearly evidence of a series of abusive attacks over

a period of time and on the day, which may have culminated in a decision by Leanne in her particularly vulnerable state to take her own life.

How and when Leanne got to the storage area, who put together the noose, who put it over the beam and in what circumstances Leanne's neck came to be in the noose, is, in the absence of an explanation from Alex O'Sachy, and in combination with the concerning matters raised in this case, leaves her final moments and that of Alex O'Sachy's involvement in what she did still uncertain.[76]

Coroner John Lock concluded that it was likely Leanne Thompson had committed suicide.

***

In 2009, Alex O'Sachy was in a relationship with a young woman, Lisa Palmos. Lisa alleged that O'Sachy liked to choke her during sex, whip her with a cat-o-nine tails and drag her around with a dress tie knotted around her neck. She alleged that O'Sachy couldn't give up drugs because every time he was straight he could see Leanne Thompson 'hanging there with her tongue out and her eyes closed'.[77]

Lisa Palmos went to police when O'Sachy grabbed her by the throat and started squeezing her neck with his hands. He pushed his fingers behind her windpipe and tried to pull it out. Lisa escaped, but when she went to have a shower, O'Sachy stabbed her in the leg.

He was arrested and charged with stabbing and assaulting her. When the case went to court, O'Sachy pleaded guilty. O'Sachy's father, George, said the allegations were false.

In 2011, O'Sachy was living with another young woman,

Lauren Howarth. Lauren grew up in Perth, and was introduced to drugs by a relative while she was still very young. In her teens she ran away from home and started using hard drugs.

In 2008, Lauren moved to Brisbane to live with her mother. It was her chance, she said, to clean up her act and make a new start in life. It is thought that Lauren met Alex O'Sachy at a methadone clinic. She moved in with him in 2010 and lived with him for about a year. It was during this time that O'Sachy was under investigation for the death of Leanne Thompson.

According to Lauren's mother, Rosina Mason-Parker, Lauren became trapped in a downward spiral of drug addiction and violence. Mrs Mason-Parker claimed that O'Sachy controlled her daughter and her money. Numerous text messages that Lauren sent her mother painted a horrific picture of the life she was leading, and the nature of her relationship with O'Sachy, including one in which she claimed he had tried to cut off her finger and had poured methylated spirits over her and threatened to set her alight.

Rosina Mason-Parker often rescued Lauren and took her home, only to despair as her daughter would stay a day or so and then return to O'Sachy.

On 1 September 2011, paramedics were called to Lauren and O'Sachy's house in Birkdale. Lauren was lying on the bed with a pillow under her head, covered by a blanket. Nearby were syringes and other drug paraphernalia. An autopsy later revealed that Lauren had died from an overdose of the prescription drug Fentanyl – an opiate that is stronger than morphine. It is believed that transdermal patches of Fentanyl were melted down to extract the drug.

George O'Sachy came to his son's defence, claiming that Alex wasn't even at home the night Lauren died. He painted her as a party girl who overdid it. George O'Sachy is on record saying he does not believe the deaths of either Lauren Howarth or Leanne Thompson were suspicious.

When Lauren's mother was handed a plastic bag that contained her daughter's earthly possessions she couldn't believe it: a packet of cigarettes, a lighter and some prescriptions. Nobody appears to know what happened to everything else Lauren owned. The O'Sachys said that was all there was.

***

The acrimonious feelings between Damian Rockett and his ex-wife Dianne Thompson have not abated over the years. She believes her daughter was murdered, he is certain it was suicide. He says Leanne was engaged in sex work, an allegation supported by Leanne's own statements to police, but the claim enrages Leanne's mother. At the inquest Damian and Dianne sat at opposite sides of the courtroom and did not acknowledge each other.

Another moment that infuriated Dianne Thompson was when Rockett invited the O'Sachy brothers to Leanne's funeral. He told journalists why he had done so. 'Well, he [Alex] had feelings for her too. And Daniel and Alex both had to get her down when she was hanging … and I thought, well they need closure too.'

Dianne Thompson was furious: 'What is he doing here?'[78]

It still grates on Dianne Thompson that after Leanne was found hanging she wasn't told right away. Damian Rockett had called his second wife, informed her of what happened and arranged to collect her from work and go straight to the hospital. It was at 4.55 p.m. that Dianne received a phone call from Child Safety, 'I presume you've heard about Leanne …'

In the hospital waiting room they couldn't bear each other's company, taking turns to sit with Leanne in intensive care until almost midnight when her life support was turned off.

And later, when George O'Sachy's wife Maria met with Damian Rockett to hand over Leanne's worldly possessions, Rockett told her, 'It [death] was the best thing that could have happened to Leanne.'[79] He said she was better off where she is now. Because of her past. And her past history. Because there was only so much he could do. Leanne was too far gone.

Rockett admitted that he hadn't seen much of his children since the end of his marriage, blaming the domestic violence order his wife had taken out on him.

Leanne Thompson was a child. A lost child. For reasons that have been strongly hinted at but never revealed, she felt it unsafe to be at home. Something happened. Whether it was her parent's nasty separation, or events that took place after that, something pushed a young, vulnerable teenager away from everything that was safe.

She squatted with friends, and sometimes with strangers. She made choices – survival choices – that she wasn't equipped to make.

Her parents knew. The Department of Child Safety knew. Schools, O'Sachy's neighbours, friends knew. Leanne was in trouble. A 15-year-old child was living with a violent, drug-using 28-year-old man. Living with him. Being fed drugs by him. Nobody stopped her. Nobody took the blame.

It's difficult to shed the image. A rag doll: stained, faded, lying limp in a corner. Too worn out to play with any more.

Cracks in the Pavement

EMMA KING
14 September 2008

Sydney's Kings Cross, the Golden Mile as it is known, is Australia's most densely populated area, with more than 20 000 people living within a 1.4-kilometre-square area. It is also the most famous red-light district in the country.

When the sun goes down over Sydney, the lights of Kings Cross come on, and the various wonders of its nightlife come out to play. Drugs are plentiful, as are strip clubs, topless waitresses, adult bookshops and loud, often aggressive spruikers inviting passers-by into tacky nightclubs.

Tourists are offered a view into the dark underbelly of Australia and its rich cross-culture of all walks of life: cross-dressers, drag queens, rich pimps with their gold chains, the poor and destitute in the gutter, and of course, more than its fair share of street-based sex workers.

Kings Cross is the place where working girls – and boys – can earn their money and spend it on their next hit without leaving the street.

It's of little surprise that a girl like Emma King, a girl who was drawn to the action, a risk-taker on a path hell-bent for self-destruction, would find the allure of Kings Cross all too appealing.

***

Emma grew up in Perth, one of two daughters of fairly wealthy parents. From the outside Emma appeared to have it all: money, a good education, the 'rich girl' lifestyle. She was well-read and very intelligent. To all appearances she seemed to have the whole world at her feet.

But appearances can be deceiving. Emma was in pain and internally she was spinning out of control. She became estranged from her parents, and with them the lifestyle to which she had been accustomed, and revealed in later years that she had been sexually abused. Though it is not clear who her abuser was, or at what age the abuse started, what is clear is that the abuse started Emma on a downhill trajectory from which there was no turning back.

Emma found heroin, a powerful narcotic that dulled the pain and replaced it with a rush of euphoria, followed by a deep nothingness where little could hurt her. Heroin wasn't enough though. Emma pushed the limits wherever she could, taking absurd risks just to feel alive. Then, more heroin, and a return to the nothing.

The cycle went on and, combined with Emma's increasing need for attention, she managed to alienate many of the people who cared about her, and pull others into the harmful spiral with her.

Emma moved around a lot, often with her current girlfriend, staying at other people's homes until their welcome had been well and truly worn out.

However, on the occasions that she was able to find her own place, she displayed some remarkably good taste. In one apartment that she shared with her partner, Ange, guests were surprised to find how pretty it was. Nothing had been purchased new but Emma had surrounded herself with an array of contrasting colours that pleased the eye. And books. Lots of books.

At this time Emma was working but would supplement that income with sex work to finance her ever-growing drug habit.

Emma and Ange's relationship was intense. One friend described them as having a 'darkness and heaviness to them both. A real sadness.' They listened to heavy music, Nine Inch Nails being one particular favourite, along with the not-so-dulcet tones of a 'very heavy-duty female thrash singer'. And yet, they could also behave with the innocent abandonment of children, running and laughing, and playing in the rain.

Emma was a tiny slip of a girl, short and petite, but Ange often said that Emma was the only person she knew who was naughtier than she was herself. An imp would be one description. This intense relationship culminated in them becoming 'blood sisters'. Each girl, with equal solemnity, cut a huge gash in the other's arm, and they mixed their blood.

Both Ange and Emma got themselves clean of drugs while they were together but that was short-lived. Neither one could resist.

Emma's need for attention and intent for self-harm accelerated. She made it known that she wanted to contract HIV and set about obtaining that goal by having unprotected sex with strangers and sharing needles with other intravenous drug users.

Emma often used emotional blackmail and the threat of self-harm to keep her girlfriends, including Ange and a previous partner, Skye, by her side. Emma made several attempts at suicide which some described as 'attention-seeking behaviour'.

At some point either Ange or Emma realised, as other girlfriends had done in the past, that they were toxic for each other and broke off their relationship.

Perhaps this was a wake-up call for Emma who then got clean

of heroin again and started making fresh plans for her future. One of these plans included moving away and making a fresh start. Perth was a relatively small place and Emma felt that because everyone knew her there, she would forever be judged.

Emma, clean of drugs and motivated for a new life, moved to Sydney. How Emma found herself in Kings Cross isn't known, but make her way there she did and it wasn't long before Emma was completely immersed in the Kings Cross culture and lifestyle. Emma made new friends and got involved in a new relationship. She also returned to her old mistress, heroin, and to sex work to pay for it.

She had a regular spot that she worked and she developed a system with her partner and a male friend to look out for her while she worked. She and her girlfriend would write down the licence plate numbers of any cars the other woman accepted a ride with. They would remain in contact via mobile phone throughout the night, and the male friend was always available to pick them up if necessary simply by text messaging him an address and pick-up time.

Such systems are commonplace amongst street-based sex workers. Each know and accept the dangers of working the streets and most quickly develop the street-smarts to sum up a potential client and possible risk level before accepting a job. However, for many, if not most, no amount of risk assessment is enough; encounters with violence are common. In a world where police protection is not expected, working girls do what they can to protect themselves and each other.

Unfortunately for Emma, no safeguards would be enough.

On the night of 13 September 2008, Emma went to work, as usual, on her patch. It was a steady night's work, so when a man approached her at around 3 a.m., Emma told him to come back in an hour. He did. Emma waved goodbye to her girlfriend and made a motion with her hand signalling that she would call soon.

Emma's friends would never see her alive again.

***

Malcolm Robert Potts was born in October 1967. At the age of 18, Potts was diagnosed with paranoid schizophrenia, a disease that is by its nature more disabling at some times than at others.

Mental illness was a common trait in Potts' family; his parents and two older siblings, a brother and a sister, also suffered from mental illness of one kind or another. In 1986, his sister suicided by shooting herself. His brother died of a drug overdose in 1991. His mother died of natural causes in 1992. It was after these deaths that the symptoms of Potts' own mental illness began to manifest.

In the years that followed, Potts was admitted and detained in psychiatric facilities on six or seven separate occasions. He was also accumulating a number of criminal convictions, mainly related to drugs. On a number of occasions, though, he was convicted of assault, and then in 1997 he was convicted of an armed robbery and given a two-year jail sentence with a nine-month minimum to be served.

In 2000, Potts was the designated carer of his father, Keith Potts, with whom he lived. One night the two had an argument, started, it is believed, by Potts' disapproval of the birthday present he was given, and Potts stabbed his father more than 30 times in what was described as a frenzied attack. Potts pleaded not guilty to murder by reason of diminished responsibility due to his mental state, and was instead found guilty of manslaughter.

Potts served his minimum term of three years and nine months and was released on parole.

Only eight months later, Potts had his parole revoked when he wrote a suggestive letter to a child; a letter that included a used condom, a photograph and money.

Potts was forced to serve out the remainder of his seven-year jail term and was once again released into the community on 4 May 2007.

Following his release, Potts was under the care of the Croydon Community Health Centre. Doctors described his condition at the time as 'chronic' and he attended the clinic fortnightly for an injection of an anti-psychotic medication. He had an injection on 4 September 2008, almost two weeks before he met Emma King.

On the night of Saturday, 13 September 2008, Potts took a train to Central Station and then walked to Kings Cross. At around 3 a.m., he approached Emma but was told to return in an hour. At about 4 a.m., Potts returned and negotiated a price of $200 with Emma for her services, and convinced her to accompany him in a taxi back to his flat.

When they arrived at the flat, Emma was greeted with a scene that would make anyone nervous: the apartment was decorated with weapons. There were tomahawks, swords and knives on the walls and on bookcases, and stacked in the corner were long sticks that had been wrapped in insulation tape.

Emma demanded payment up-front. With so many weapons close at hand she couldn't be sure that Potts would pay *after* he received her services.

Potts went to the kitchen, presumably to get the promised cash. However, it was discovered later that there was little more than $100 in Potts' home – not enough to cover the agreed fee.

Potts later asserted that in the kitchen he heard a voice warning him to be 'careful of her'. Whether because of the voice, or because he realised he was unable to pay, when Potts returned from the kitchen he told Emma that he'd changed his mind and wanted her to leave.

Emma was understandably angry and upset. Potts had wasted her time, and in Emma's world time meant money. Emma called her friend, and at the same time hurled abuse at Potts.

'No one fucks me around,' she allegedly said, according to Potts. 'My friends are coming. You either produce the money or we're taking your stuff.'[80]

Emma asked Potts for the address and at 4.26 a.m. her friend received a text message to pick Emma up from Unit 5/24 Margaret Street, Ashfield. But Potts had deliberately given Emma the wrong address to confuse her friends and prolong the time they had together.

Potts' demeanour had changed noticeably and Emma backed against a bookcase calling her friends continuously, wondering why they hadn't arrived to pick her up yet. Potts paced the floor, paranoid about the 'warning' he'd received about Emma and growing increasingly agitated.

He was 187 centimetres tall and weighed 118 kilograms; the much smaller Emma felt threatened. She was only 162 centimetres tall and weighed barely 55 kilograms – less than half his weight.

According to Potts, she picked up a knife from the shelf behind her and said, 'Fuck you, you fat prick, come near me I'll fucken stab ya.'

Potts told Emma to drop the knife but there was no way she was going to do that. This guy looked crazy – and he was big. She just needed to hold him off until her friends arrived. *Where were they?*

Potts flew into a rage. He threw his considerable weight at Emma, tackling her to the floor and knocking the knife from her hand. On her stomach, and fearing for her life, Emma reached for the knife that lay tantalisingly close in front of her. Potts dived on her back and pinned her, face down, to the floor with his body weight. He reached forward and picked up the discarded knife. Then, using all the strength that his size and his rage afforded him, Potts raised the knife in the air and plunged it deep into Emma's back. One of the wounds penetrated the full length of the blade – 33 centimetres – passing through vital organs and ending Emma's life.

But Potts wasn't finished yet, even now that Emma's ordeal was over. While Emma's friends still drove up and down Margaret Street in Ashfield searching frantically for number 24, a number that didn't exist, Potts busied himself stripping the clothes from Emma's lifeless body. He dragged the dead woman into his bedroom and laid her on his bed, then had sexual intercourse with her corpse, leaving his semen in her vagina.

Potts then 'hid' Emma under his bed and made an attempt to clean up the evidence, even going so far as to paint over some, but not all, of the bloodstains with white paint. He bagged up Emma's clothes, shoes and few possessions, and carried them to an adjacent apartment building where he disposed of them in neighbours' bins.

Emma's partner and friends spent the morning frantically trying to reach her, their fear for her safety escalating with every unanswered phone call and every passing minute. They began doorknocking every home and apartment in Margaret Street, which they found only went up to number 12 – not 24 – the address they'd been given. Nobody knew where Emma was.

However, while waiting outside the apartment block at number 12, Emma's partner saw a face peering out of the window of an apartment where it had been apparent that nobody was home – or not answering. She called the police, reporting Emma's uncharacteristic disappearance and her suspicions about *that* apartment.

Police arrived on-scene around midday and forced their way into the apartment. There stood Potts with a knife in each hand demanding to know who was going to fix the door the police had just broken. It didn't take long before Emma's body was found and Potts was duly arrested and charged with her murder.

Despite Potts pleading not guilty by reason of self-defence, a jury convicted him of murder, rejecting the idea that a man twice the size of the victim would need to stab her *in the back* to defend himself.

Emma's sister and partner each tendered victim impact statements during the sentencing hearing, both poignantly describing the shattering effect Emma's death had had upon them and family members.

The court considered the aggravated nature of Potts' behaviour following her death, his psychiatric history, as well as his lengthy criminal record, in making a decision.

Justice David Kirby concluded that Potts unquestionably represented a 'high risk of further violent crime', and imposed a prison term of 28 years, with a minimum of 21 to be served before he is eligible for parole.

***

One has to question both our legal system and the state of our mental health system that Malcolm Robert Potts was a free man in 2008 and able to commit this crime against Emma King. Given his long criminal record – including the stabbing death of his father, along with other violent crimes – and the psychiatrist treating Potts' assessment that his schizophrenia was 'chronic', why was there no intervention?

Potts said himself in court that the anti-psychotic drugs he was being injected with every two weeks were necessary to sedate him because 'I am big and aggressive'.[81]

And yet this big, aggressive, mentally unstable, violent offender was left unchecked to claim another victim.

'JENNY' & 'SUSAN'
November 2008

'Jenny' and 'Susan' arrived in Sydney, Australia, on 6 September 2008, part of a tour group led by China Merchants International Travel. Within hours they had disappeared. They were reported missing to the Department of Immigration on 8 September. Jenny was married and Susan was a widow with an eight-year-old daughter. Both women were in their 30s and it was later discovered they had stayed to work as freelance sex workers in a number of brothels. The women had sublet a tiny partitioned room in an overcrowded apartment in Auburn.

Two months later, on 13 November, the decomposing bodies of the women were found on their bed. Their throats had been cut. Police said the attack was so horrific they could not use photos to help with the identification of the women. Despite the fact that 11 other people lived in the apartment nobody knew, saw or heard anything. The day the bodies were discovered, a pimp was heard boasting about their deaths. Yet their murders remain unsolved.

She's Over There
REBECCA APPS
9 September 2010

When Mr Ryan decided to do some work in his backyard one morning, he had not a care in the world. It was around 8 a.m. on 9 September 2010. He was pottering away when he heard strange noises on the other side of his fence. As his property backed onto a bushland reserve at Oak Flats, near Port Kembla in New South Wales, and most of the noises he usually heard at this time of day came from wildlife, his curiosity was piqued.

He bent down and tried to have a sneaky peek through the cracks in his fence palings. He couldn't see properly, but the sounds and the glimpses of something bizarre had aroused his curiosity. He could tell there was a car parked very close to his fence, but he couldn't make out what was going on. Mr Ryan found a milk crate to give himself a better view.

He blinked. He was stunned. The car was a Hyundai Excel hatchback, and he watched in horror as a man tried to pull a limp, motionless body from the back seat. He saw a man grab the partially naked body and start dragging it backwards. He grabbed his phone, crouched down and dialled triple-0.

The man was still there when police arrived. He was sitting in his car with the door open.

Sergeant Smith: 'What are you doing?'

David Dunn: 'Nothing.'

Sergeant Smith: 'Where is she?'

David Dunn: 'I don't know.'

Sergeant Smith: 'I'm going to ask you again and if you lie, I'm going to break your fucking nose.'

David Dunn: 'She is under the tin over there.'

Sergeant Smith: 'Is she alive?'

David Dunn: 'No.'[82]

Sergeant Smith ran to the ditch and lifted the tin. He discovered a lifeless young woman, naked, tucked into a foetal position, with significant amounts of blood around her nose and mouth.

There was grass over her body. Dunn admitted he had thrown it over her in the hope it would soak up some of the blood.

***

Wentworth Street, Port Kembla, was known as a place to go to pick up sex workers or score drugs. On any given day there were up to 20 street-based sex workers, many of whom were homeless, and most selling sex to buy heroin.

Rebecca Apps worked there under the alias 'Crystal'. She was a 28-year-old woman who had relinquished custody of her sons to her own mother as she became enslaved to heroin.

By 2010, Rebecca had reconnected with her family after a long absence. She was thrilled to be back in touch with her boys, and friends said it was all she could talk about. She wanted things to change. She wanted to clean up her life and become more involved with her family.

As a child growing up on the NSW south coast, Rebecca had a stable, loving family. According to friends she was really smart, although she went to some trouble to hide it, and she was a gifted, trained singer with a beautiful voice. She got in with 'the wrong crowd', left her children with her family and drifted away.

Where did she go? Nobody seems to know a lot about that. Her new family became the people on the streets who understood her plight, the customers with whom she exchanged services for money, and the dealers who swapped that money for drugs. Addiction isn't easy. Life on the streets isn't easy either. But addiction is the master that overrides everything else, and when a woman has to feed a need that costs anywhere between $300 and $1500 a day, she will sometimes get into a car with a man when her instincts are screaming at her to walk away. Rebecca had been working the streets of Port Kembla for about a year when she agreed to get into a car with David Dunn.

***

The night before he killed Rebecca, David Dunn used a toma-hawk to commit an armed robbery that netted him $85. He had been on an ice bender.

Ice. A methamphetamine that looks like someone has shaved shards from an ice cube. Heat it up, liquefy it, then smoke, snort or inject it and – boom! In less than 10 seconds you feel amazing, bulletproof, alert, confident, focused. It has hit the brain's pleasure centre and released up to 1000 times the normal amount of dopamine. It also releases noradrenaline, the 'fight or flight' chemical that makes your heart beat faster, your breathing more rapid and your pupils expand. Palms might feel sweaty, you want to bounce on your feet, you're ready for anything.

Too much ice, too often, makes you anxious. You grind your teeth, struggle to sleep, pick at imaginary sores, lose interest in food. Become edgy. Depressed. Irritable. Then nasty.

And you've lost that great feeling; the one that made you bulletproof. You need more.

David Dunn was on day 12 of a bender when he picked Rebecca Apps up. According to him, she asked if he would take her to her heroin dealer and he agreed to do it. Nobody will ever know what transpired that morning, except that Rebecca got into the car he was driving (which he had stolen) and they drove to the back of a service station. Rebecca took off her denim skirt in anticipation of the sexual service she was about to offer, and Dunn attacked her with a tomahawk. She was lying on the ground when the attack began. Rebecca screamed and begged for her life, but it made no difference. He beat her until she was dead.

He would later offer a number of different stories about why he had murdered Rebecca. One story, told in his initial interview, was that he was embarrassed and frustrated by his impotence. Then he changed it. This time, while he was having sex with Rebecca he noticed tattoos on her ankle. He got confused and thought he was with his ex-wife who, he alleged, had killed their children. And in a completely new story, he told police he hadn't meant to kill her, he just wanted to shut her up.

The court heard that Rebecca Apps died from a head injury. She had suffered multiple complex wounds to her head which were consistent with blows from an axe. There was significant fracturing of the skull. Toxicological tests revealed that there were benzodiazepines, cannabis, alcohol and methamphetamines in Rebecca's bloodstream – none of which contributed to her death.

Justice Christine Adamson was moved by the case. She fought back tears when she tried to sum up the case and give her reasons for the sentence she was about to impose. She sentenced 29-year-old Dunn to 21 years in prison, with a minimum of 14 years.

'The death of the deceased was brought about by lack of

tolerance and frustration, which was brought on by the drugs he had taken,' she said. 'The method of killing was particularly violent and carried out in complete disregard for the deceased's pleas for mercy … Her last minutes of life must have been spent in terror, horrific pain and despair.'[83]

Justice Adamson also suggested he seek drug rehabilitation while he was incarcerated.

Rebecca's' mother, Christine Bennett, told Dunn's sentence hearing the light went out of her life when she heard her daughter had been murdered. 'David, I don't know why you did what you did. I probably never will,' Christine Bennett spoke to her daughter's murderer. 'But you have taken away one of the greatest treasures God ever gave to me.'

Rebecca's sister, Heather Bennett, had been unable to view her sister's body after the brutal attack. 'David Dunn took away my last goodbye,' Heather Bennett said. 'My sister was an amazing, beautiful, delightful person and should be here today.'[84]

The murder of Rebecca Apps was senseless and cruel. In some ways, so was the terrible reality of the way drug addiction kidnapped her potential to become the mother, the woman she wanted to be. She didn't deserve to be murdered and her family, who knew and loved her, did not deserve to be broken. But they were.

SHUXIA YUAN
5 December 2010

On 5 December 2010, 52-year-old Shuxia Yuan was murdered by 18-year-old James William Glenn, in a motel room in Gladstone, Queensland.

Stabbed 23 times with a fishing knife and with her throat cut, Shuxia managed to crawl to the front door of her motel room and open it, desperately seeking help.

Witnesses tried to rush her to hospital but only got as far as the motel parking lot before Shuxia, with several major arteries severed, collapsed from the massive blood loss and died.

The murder was described in court as an 'inexplicable crime' and a display of 'savagery'[85]. Her killer, Glenn, planned the crime after he saw an advertisement for sex workers in the classifieds section of a local newspaper. Glenn purchased the weapon used in the attack the very morning of the murder.

Despite pleading not guilty to murder, but instead to the lesser crime of manslaughter because he hadn't intended to kill Shuxia, Glenn was convicted of murder by a jury and sentenced to life in prison, with a minimum of 25 years to serve.

VALMAI BIRCH
22 March 2011

Valmai Jane Birch was 34 years old at the time of her murder. She lived in a townhouse in the North Wollongong suburb of Woonona and neighbours had become used to the sounds of arguing and screaming that would often come from behind her walls. So when they heard the sound of 'something more than a scream', they ignored it. Their neighbour made them feel uncomfortable, and they decided they didn't want to get involved.

It was a few weeks later, on 22 March, when the stench coming from her flat became unbearable, that they called the police. When police broke in they discovered Valmai's badly decomposing body stuffed in a wheelie bin in her bathroom. To date, the murder remains unsolved.

Valmai Birch is survived by two sons.

JOHANNA MARTIN
11 October 2011

Johanna Martin is a name known to few, though thousands of Australians have probably been privy to one of her shows, or engaged in sex with her, either in public or private.

Johanna was known as Honie to those who knew and loved her – and there were many. She was married for more than 40 years, mother to a son, Wayne, and a daughter, Paulene. She was known as Nanna to her grandchildren.

People recognised the rich socialite, garishly dressed and dripping in gold, coming and going from her home at the Docklands in Melbourne in her luxury convertible Mercedes Benz.

Even more people though knew the name, the persona, that she became at night: Jazzy O – Australia's most famous and daring stripper and sex worker.

When Jazzy O was murdered, Johanna was forgotten by the media who flew into a frenzy of salacious details about her performing life, speculating on her death being related to her sex work – it must have been a sex game gone wrong.

Even her killer, motivated by greed more than anything else, capitalised on this angle, using the media's creation as his own defence at his murder trial.

For the media, Johanna never existed. For Honie's family and friends, it was Jazzy O who never existed. It wasn't a stripper or a sex worker who was murdered. It was Johanna. Mum. Nanna.

***

Johanna was born in Holland and, with her family, moved to Australia when she was just four years old. She grew up in the manner typical of a girl in post-war Australia. As a teenager, she met Arthur Martin and in 1963, when Johanna was 17, the two were married in a church in Richmond, Victoria.

Arthur and Johanna lived a simple life in Powelltown, a tiny timber-industry town in the Yarra State Forest. Here Johanna took great delight in creating a cosy home for the two children she would birth. She grew her own vegetables and made her own clothes.

Life was not always great with Arthur, however. No matter how hard Johanna tried, no matter how much she did, he was prone to outbursts of rage – often violent.

Johanna decided she needed something outside of her marriage and children to satisfy her and to make her own money so as not to have to rely on her controlling and abusive husband for her every need.

The idea for Jazzy O was born. Johanna talked of the creation of Jazzy O with a friend: 'She told me that she'd seen some strip shows and heard comments coming from the audience that they were boring. She thought that she could perform much better and do more interesting shows and make a lot of money out of it.'[86]

And boy, was she right.

Jazzy O prided herself on doing what others wouldn't. She

was determined that no matter what another act could promise, she would deliver something bigger, better and more outrageous. Her show became the 'must see' strip show, with bookings coming months in advance for bucks nights and end-of-year sporting club events.

Jazzy O was on the books with several elite escort agencies, as well as taking her own bookings – no one was in charge of Jazzy O but herself. And nobody ever walked away disappointed with her show. She really was more daring and outrageous than anyone else, just as she said. She used props such as fruits and vegetables – and even witches hats – on stage, and even performed live sex acts with members of the audience.

There wasn't much Jazzy O wouldn't do; group sex was a specialty. But everyone who knew her said she drew the line at bondage. Allowing somebody to tie her up left her too vulnerable and that was something she could not tolerate. One friend said that Jazzy was too afraid somebody would steal her (very expensive) jewellery while she was tied up.

Barbara Bushell, owner of one of the escort agencies Jazzy worked for, and her friend, testified in court the reasons for Jazzy's reluctance to be involved in bondage. She said it was a fear stemming from actions by her husband, Arthur. According to Barbara, 'One time he got a strap and tried to strap her hands together. She was too frightened, crying and screaming ... He hit her but he stopped. She would never allow anybody to tie her up, because of what she went through with Arthur.'[87]

As Jazzy O, Johanna accumulated a small fortune. With assets including a holiday house and her apartment at Southbank, her luxury convertible Mercedes, and the gold she was permanently draped in, Johanna is reported to have been worth in excess of $3.5 million. She was such a regular customer at the Mercedes dealership that a staff member actually attended her funeral.

But when the makeup was scrubbed from her face and the costumes hung in her wardrobe, Johanna was Honie again, mother and grandmother, who kept the secrets of her work from many in her family.

One of her son Wayne's friends from school was a regular visitor to their home and only found out that Jazzy O and Wayne's mum, Mrs Martin, were the same person when he saw the headlines in a newspaper and recognised her from the accompanying photo. She had just been his mate's mum, a little flamboyant maybe, but always ready for a quick word and some after-school treats.

On Father's Day in 2010, Arthur died. After more than four decades of marriage, Johanna was alone. She wouldn't let that get her down though. In fact, quite the opposite. She relished being her own woman and vowed never to have to answer to anyone again. She wasn't interested in another relationship, she said.

***

In early 2011, Johanna was at the South Melbourne Market, a place she frequented, when she overheard a man talking about his daughter doing extras work on television. This piqued Johanna's interest – she'd long had a dream of doing something similar, in particular appearing on one of her favourite TV shows, Australian drama *Neighbours*.

Johanna approached the man and asked about any contacts he might have for people in the industry. The two struck up a conversation and exchanged phone numbers. It was the beginning of a friendship that would culminate in Johanna's death.

Steve Constantinou was a 49-year-old, self-employed handyman. At the time of meeting Johanna, he had a serious gambling addiction and owed a large sum of money – in excess of \$60 000 – to the Sheriff's Office for unpaid fines.

It's likely that he viewed the older, single, much wealthier woman as a meal ticket.

Constantinou and Johanna were regularly seen out and about together, and Johanna often joked with her friends about the younger man who was very good at spending her money.

On several occasions Johanna and Constantinou attended the bank together, each time Johanna withdrawing sums of money which she reportedly lent to Constantinou to pay off his debts. He later admitted that most of the money was spent gambling, though he claimed that the sums of money were gifts.

This was out of character for Johanna. She certainly liked the good things in life and wasn't afraid to spend money. Good friend Adrian Ciarrocchi talked of how Johanna loved the theatre and always bought 'the best A-row seats'.[88] However, she wasn't in the habit of giving handouts to anyone, not even her own children. She believed that she'd worked for every cent she had, and that everybody else should do the same. On the rare occasion that she did loan money, it was always with the understanding that it would be repaid.

Constantinou was drowning deeply in debt. He could see no way to pay the money back; he became desperate and a plot formed in his mind.

On the night of 10 October 2011, Jazzy O left home and worked a shift at a West Melbourne brothel, Images. It was a quiet night with Jazzy seeing only two clients, both men who'd walked in off the street. It was the kind of night that made Jazzy wish she'd stayed at home.

She returned home late, scrubbed Jazzy away, and went to bed. The following morning, Johanna dressed in three-quarter-length pants, a maroon singlet, a grey jacket, high heeled shoes and a red beret-style hat. Her usual array of gold jewellery, including bracelets, necklaces, and rings for every finger, was draped over her. Johanna was never one to leave the house without standing out from the crowd.

Johanna collected her mobile phone and handbag, and her little Jack Russell, Suzie, who she took almost everywhere, and drove off in her Mercedes Benz convertible at about 9.50 a.m. At 10.07 a.m., Johanna called Steve Constantinou. The content of that conversation is unknown, but it was certainly the last phone call Johanna ever made.

Around lunchtime, Steve Constantinou attended a Bunnings store in Port Melbourne and then returned to his apartment in Port Melbourne.

Johanna arrived at the apartment and Constantinou greeted her and let her in. At some point in the next hour, he surprised Johanna, coming up behind her with some sort of ligature, possibly a rope, and strangled her.

He then stripped Johanna's body of all of her jewellery, left her body where it was, and around 1 p.m. drove to a pawnbroker's premises in Footscray. There he pawned the gold necklaces, bangles and rings for a sum of $2100. According to the pawnbroker, to whom Constantinou was a regular customer, he seemed no different that afternoon than he had on any other occasion. Nothing seemed to be out of the usual in his behaviour.

Constantinou then returned to his apartment where he wrapped a sheet around Johanna's body, tied a rope around it, and put her in his car. He then drove a short distance to an industrial area of Port Melbourne, parked his car in the street and dragged Johanna's body across the road where he discarded her on the nature strip. Johanna's body was discovered about an hour later.

He returned home once again, arriving at his apartment at 2.10 p.m. Soon after, he set off from his apartment once again, this time to a TAB at the Clare Castle Hotel in Port Melbourne where he placed a $10 000 bet. According to his evidence, part of this sum was the money he'd received at the pawnbroker's early that afternoon.

Again Constantinou returned home, only to go out again a short time later, this time to the Rex Hotel in Port Melbourne where he said he had to collect on a bet. It is unknown if this was related to the bet he'd placed earlier that day or a preceding one.

About 3.30 p.m., Constantinou took his car to a Beaurepaires store in Port Melbourne where he had new tyres fitted. He left the store at 4.12 p.m.

Again, Constantinou returned home. This time he collected Johanna's handbag and car keys and drove her Mercedes, with her little dog Suzie still in it, about three quarters of a kilometre away, where he left it. The car was discovered two days later with Suzie still inside and luckily still alive.

In total, Constantinou left his apartment on six occasions on the afternoon that he'd killed Johanna: first, to attend the pawnbroker; second, to dispose of Johanna's body; third, to place a bet; fourth, to collect winnings; fifth, to have his car tyres changed; and sixth, to move Johanna's car. At no point during those six outings did Constantinou appear to behave oddly; there was nothing to indicate that this was a man who'd just killed someone who he'd supposedly considered a friend. So when he later claimed to police and to the courts that he'd been involved in a sexual relationship with Johanna and that her death had been an accident, one that he'd panicked about, his story was a little hard to swallow.

***

Johanna's funeral was held at the Fawkner Memorial Park and was well attended and appropriately moving. Family and friends gathered to pay tribute to the 'infectious spirit' of the woman known as Honie. She was remembered for her love of 'laughter and enjoyment and family caring time together'.[89] Grieving together were family and friends of Johanna, and those in the sex industry who knew and loved Jazzy O, but amidst talk of how hard working she was, there was no mention of the industry she was in. The family either didn't know or chose not to acknowledge Jazzy O – instead they focused on the woman, the mother, the grandmother and friend.

It was a family wracked with grief, sobs filling the chapel while a slideshow played favourite pictures from the 65-year-old's full life. Hers was a life that mattered to many and she would be sorely missed. The one thing that many were thinking, but nobody said out loud, was their desperate need for Johanna's killer to be brought to justice.

***

Steve Constantinou was interviewed by police several times and each time his story about what had happened to Johanna changed. Then, when he went to trial for her murder, pleading not guilty, he concocted a story, most likely planted in his mind by the media's suggestions that it was a sex game gone wrong. He ran with that idea, stating that Johanna had enjoyed bondage and on the day she died, she'd put a dog collar around her neck and asked him to pull on the reins that were attached to it. According to Constantinou she kept demanding that he pull tighter and tighter and at some point she slumped forward and he slumped on top of her. It was only later that he realised she was dead and then he panicked, which caused him to get rid of her body and any evidence that she'd been in his apartment.

Forensic pathologist Dr Paul Bedford, who conducted the

post-mortem examination of Johanna, observed bruising and extensive bleeding around her main neck muscles, consistent with force having to be applied for at least 30 seconds. Abrasions around the neck also indicated that there was probably some resistance during the strangulation. He opined that it was impossible for somebody to strangle herself to death the way Constantinou had said it had happened. And, he added, the strangulation had gone on for a good length of time after Johanna would have passed out. All this made Constantinou's version of events very unlikely.

Several witnesses also gave evidence about Johanna's dislike for any form of bondage, and the fact that she'd denied having a sexual relationship with Constantinou. She enjoyed just having a friend, she'd told them, and joked that she'd had enough sex in her lifetime to last her.

The prosecutor called Constantinou out on every lie, on every change to his story since his initial police interview, casting serious doubt on any credibility he may have had. At one point during the trial the prosecutor asked, 'So you killed her?'

Constantinou answered, 'Without intent. It was an accident and I don't like the fact that you are saying I killed her, I don't like that.'

The prosecutor hit back with, 'Hang around, because I am going to tell this jury you're guilty of murder.'[90]

It was the one light moment in what was a long, arduous trial.

The jury dismissed Constantinou's version of what happened and found him guilty of murder. In sentencing Constantinou, the judge said, 'The various journeys which the appellant made on the afternoon of the killing were ordered, and bespoke no confusion. The appellant's disposition, as observed and observable, bespoke no distress. The appellant's apparent callousness knew no bounds.'[90]

Victim impact statements were provided to the court by Johanna's son Wayne, her daughter Paulene, her grandchildren Katrina and Sam, and various extended family and friends. Each described the 'kind, funny, gregarious, engaging, loving and much-loved individual, whose death has affected adversely the lives of many who will greatly miss her'.

In his sentencing speech, Justice Phillip Priest said Constantinou had run a 'scurrilous defence, underpinned by the blatantly preposterous claim that Ms Martin had met her death in the course of a sex game gone wrong. It was a somewhat opportunistic attempt, in my opinion, to capitalise on the fact that Ms Martin was a sex worker ... You strangled Ms Martin from behind, in such a position and with sufficient force that she was unable to resist you ... I detect in you no shred of remorse.'[92]

Justice Priest went on to sentence Constantinou to 24 years in prison, with a non-parole period of 20 years.

Since sentencing, Constantinou has made several attempts to have his case reheard, always insisting on his innocence, but nobody's buying it. These were the actions of a greedy man, in over his head, a man who rather than feel remorseful, immediately went about the business of destroying evidence and making money from his victim.

The story of Jazzy O was a titillating one for reporters for a few days. It had all the hallmarks of a scandal: 'Australia's Oldest Sex Worker. Death Caused By Sex Game Gone Wrong'. However, once the truth was revealed, and the woman behind the facade was seen to be a real woman and a victim, the media interest waned. Jazzy O is still a legend in the industry. But to her family, Jazzy O was merely a means to an end. They knew the real Johanna. Their beloved Honie. Mum. Nanna. It's a pity everybody else seemed to forget about her.

The Blood-Soaked Sofa
DEBARA MARTIN
3 May 2012

Sex work can be a dangerous occupation, that much is obvious. On the streets a worker is vulnerable and must rely on her street-smarts and intuition to sum up a situation quickly and make a decision whether a client is going to be your average john, serviced, paid and gone, or if there is something more sinister lurking. Robberies, rapes and violence are, sadly, commonplace and there's the ever-present threat of a monster on the prowl for a victim, for someone who is easy prey to satisfy their bloodlust.

But not all predators are strangers stalking the night. Sometimes a predator is closer than that. Sometimes he's in your own home. Sharing your bed. Sometimes he's the same person who tells you he loves you.

Such was the case with Debara Martin who was savagely murdered in her own home by her own boyfriend.

Yet the headlines, the few that there were, still insisted on using the term prostitute to describe the victim, and toy boy to describe the much younger perpetrator, despite there being nothing about those two facts that informed the public of the circumstances of the murder, much less excused it.

***

Debara Martin was New Zealand born and raised. Her life had none of the hallmarks of many of the other girls in the sex industry. Her family talk of her 'beautiful spirit', her loving nature and her ambition.

When Debara left school she worked hard as an apprentice and eventually earned her trade certificate as a qualified chef. But times were hard, opportunities scarce, and as a young mother, it was often difficult to make ends meet. Debara used sex work as a way to supplement her income. Without the usual trappings of homelessness or drug abuse so common to sex workers, Debara was able to move in and out of the trade at will.

In 2010, Debara took the bold step of relocating from her home in New Zealand to Australia. Tempted by the allure of greater employment opportunities and a fresh start, Debara reasoned it could be the beginning of a whole new life.

She set up home in a small town, Bowraville, in New South Wales, where she found that sex work was the easiest and most profitable way to earn her living.

It was during her time as a sex worker in 2011 that she first met Adam John Kennedy. Despite an age difference of nearly 20 years – she was 42 and he only 23 – the two hit it off and became a couple. Debara would joke about their relationship, often referring to Kennedy as her toy boy.

Debara gave up sex work and gained employment as a kitchen hand in a cafe in Coffs Harbour, a job she apparently enjoyed but which didn't pay nearly the same amounts that she was used to earning in the sex industry. Sometimes she would talk about returning to her previous work, a suggestion Kennedy vehemently disagreed with.

Debara had a wide circle of friends and was popular at work

with her kindness and quick wit. Close friend, Eve Whakatutu described her: 'She was a hard worker and loved being a chef. She was beautiful – so free-spirited and golden-hearted. You always knew where she was because she had a laugh that everyone would remember.'[93]

When Debara was diagnosed with breast cancer, friends rallied around her. She underwent a mastectomy and was in the process of undergoing reconstructive surgery but she never let that get her down. She had, she reasoned, beaten cancer, she could battle anything.

An online tribute read: 'She was a beautiful soul, vivacious, warm, energetic, friendly and irrepressible, just having had a breast removed from cancer. She was still having reconstructive surgery. She was a battler and never afraid of hard work and for this to have happened to her is just the worst kind of wrong imaginable.'[94]

***

Adam Kennedy had a serious drinking problem. Alcoholism had plagued him since his teens. At times he was able to put the drink aside for a while but it never lasted. Work would become too hard or life too complicated and he would walk away and hit the bottle.

Kennedy's parents separated when he was 12 and he left school before completing year 9. Initially he was employed by his mother working in a nursery but when she formed a new relationship and moved to Queensland, Kennedy refused to go, preferring instead to remain in New South Wales, unemployed and without a fixed address.

When he was 19, he moved back in with his father and returned to study at TAFE with the intention of obtaining his school certificate. This attempt was quickly unsuccessful and Kennedy abandoned his studies.

Not long after, he gained employment as a process worker and later as a forklift driver but he was unable to hold down a job for any length of time due to his excessive drinking.

He obtained an apprenticeship as a cabinet maker then returned to his job as a process worker but routinely spent all of his wages on alcohol. The pattern was set. He needed the job to drink but he couldn't work because he was too drunk.

In early 2012, Debara Martin noticed changes in Kennedy's behaviour. He had become increasingly short-tempered and prone to fits of alcohol-fuelled rage. He was drinking more and could not be convinced to slow down.

Debara complained to a number of friends that Kennedy had become violent towards her but she was reluctant to call the police.

At the end of March, a drunken Kennedy held a knife to Debara's throat, threatening her. Still she could not be convinced to alert authorities.

Shortly before her death in May, Debara was observed to have a black eye and a swollen face, injuries inflicted by Kennedy. Debara decided enough was enough and told Kennedy it was over. She told friends that the two had split up but it was difficult for her to move on. She knew this wasn't the real Adam, the one she'd fallen in love with. Maybe she could help him to stop drinking and he – and they – would be all right again.

Adam Kennedy drank almost continuously for the next few weeks.

On 3 May 2012, Kennedy sat at a local hotel bar drinking all day while Debara was at work. At around 5 p.m. she arrived at the hotel looking for him and they returned to the house they shared in Toormina, a suburb of Coffs Harbour. Immediately,

Kennedy saw that his belongings had been packed and had been placed out the front.

Despite all of his promises it had become clear to Debara that nothing was going to change. When she had arrived home from work expecting Kennedy to keep his promise to take her out somewhere nice for dinner that night, and found that he was out on another drinking bender, she'd had it. Debara had packed his bags.

Debara and Kennedy argued, and he became increasingly agitated while Debara became visibly upset. Eventually, exhausted, Debara agreed to let Kennedy stay, on the condition that he stop drinking.

Kennedy convinced Debara to go and have a lie down and a sleep so that she would feel better. While she slept, Kennedy slipped out and purchased a bottle of rum.

Debara woke up and bleary-eyed and groggy from sleep, wandered into their living area to find Kennedy drinking – only hours after they'd argued and reconciled.

Angry, she ordered him from the house. Kennedy refused. The two argued and the altercation became more and more volatile. Kennedy asserted that she threatened to stab him and at one point squeezed his testicles, but there is no evidence to either support or refute his claims. It may be a case of trying to diminish his sense of responsibility for what he did next.

Kennedy's rage was blind. He punched Debara and punched her again. And again. His fist connected with her face, snapping her head sideways, then another punch with the other fist to knock it back the other way. Over and over he pummelled her in the face, chest and abdomen.

Debara raised her arms to fend off the blows but he was too strong. He sat heavily on top of her, causing blunt force trauma to her abdomen, and continued to punch her. Blood flowed from her mouth and nose, and from other cuts and abrasions. Eventually Debara lost consciousness and stopped struggling. Still it's unlikely from the amount of damage done that Kennedy immediately noticed – or stopped his beating, such was his rage.

Finally spent, Kennedy stopped and realised what he'd done. He bundled Debara into his car and drove away.

At about 11.30 p.m., Luke Kennedy, Adam's brother, awoke in his Tewinga home – around 38 kilometres south of Toormina – to the sound of knocking and screaming at his door. Alarmed, he staggered out of bed and found his brother stumbling and heavily intoxicated. 'I've killed her ... I finally killed her,' he slurred.[95]

Brendan Ware, a friend of the brothers, was asleep in a bedroom in the back of the house when he heard the screaming and yelling. Making his way to the living room in front of the house, he saw Adam 'off his fucking head' and saying things about killing someone in 'drunken rampage mumbles'.[96] Brendan had seen Adam drunk before, and knew he was prone to violent outbursts, but he'd never seen him quite this drunk. Frightened, Brendan ran away and hid in a nearby paddock.

At this point, Adam asked Luke to help him dispose of the body. Horrified, Luke refused and Adam left the house. He returned a short time later, carrying Debara's body, which he unceremoniously dumped on Luke's couch and once again left the house, this time driving away.

Brendan heard the sound of the engine gunning to life, and Adam driving away, and made his way back across the paddock and into the house. As he entered, he saw a person's bloodied leg hanging over the end of the sofa. He didn't wait around to see who it was or what had happened; he took off and stayed at a friend's house.

Subsequently, Luke saw Debara lying on the sofa. He noticed

blood dripping from her head, injuries to her face and a white substance that he thought was something like moisturiser on her head. Luke knew without further investigation that Debara was dead.

Luke collected some clothing from his bedroom and left the house. As he left, he noticed some items of clothing strewn around outside on the ground where his brother had parked his car earlier. Luke got into his own car and drove to the Macksville Police Station, arriving there at around 3 a.m., where he reported the incident.

Half an hour earlier, at 2.30 a.m., police noticed a car travelling at excessive speed in a southerly direction along the Pacific Highway near Taree. Police had received reports earlier of a similar car swerving across the road erratically. They pulled the car over and the offender fled on foot. Police gave chase and apprehended him, noting immediately that he smelt strongly of alcohol, his speech was slurred, he was unsteady on his feet and he was only partially dressed. They took the man into custody and ascertained that his name was Adam John Kennedy.

Meanwhile, police had taken Luke's statement and had arrived at his home in Tewinga where they discovered Debara's body. She was wearing a short black skirt, a singlet-type top which was pushed up revealing her stomach and a pink bra, and ankle-length socks. She was not wearing shoes and when police moved her body, they found a baseball bat beneath her.

Police noted that the left side of Debara's face was heavily bruised and swollen, and blood was draining from her mouth and nose. Her hair was soaked with blood and her denture plate was tangled in her hair. She had blood on both hands, both arms, both feet and her right thigh.

Bizarrely, police also noticed a white cream substance on Debara's face, and an empty 375-millilitre tube of hair conditioner rested near her face. The same white cream was found in an oval shape on the floor and another pattern of it on the bottom sheet of Luke's bed.

Police then moved on to the murder scene itself, the home that Debara and Adam had shared. There they found that a clear oily residue had been sprayed over the inside of the front door, the kitchen floor was wet with soil scattered across it along with several footprints, blue marker pen had been used to scribble on the front of the refrigerator door, inside the refrigerator a symbol had been drawn in tomato sauce, a potted plant and soil had been tipped into and around the bowl of the bathroom vanity, another pot containing soil was in the toilet bowl along with a can of air freshener, a tube of toothpaste had been used to scrawl 'BW' and 'AK' on the vanity, and the words 'On Dave' had been written in purple soap on the sliding doors of the vanity.

Police were shocked with their discoveries – the brutality of the attack on Debara was bad enough, but the bizarre nature of the rest of the crime scenes was disturbing.

Adam John Kennedy was subsequently charged with Debara Martin's murder.

In court, Professor Lyons presented the findings of the autopsy he performed on Debara. Her injuries were horrific. Debara had sustained incredibly painful injuries inflicted over an excruciating length of time. Most of the wounds were consistent with having been caused by vigorous blows from Kennedy's fists, although experts couldn't rule out the use of a weapon, such as the baseball bat found under Debara's body, for some of the injuries. Professor Lyons also made reference to the fact that some of the injuries could have been 'caused by a weapon in the sense of a shoe in stamping'.[97]

So complex were the pattern of injuries to Debara's body

that it was not possible to describe any one particular event as being the terminal one. Any one of the injuries could have been the fatal blow.

Andrew John Kennedy pleaded guilty to Debara's murder and was subsequently convicted. In sentencing Kennedy, the court had to consider that he was not of good moral character prior to the crime, having previous criminal convictions for violent crime. Kennedy's pleas to seek help with his alcoholism and claims that he could be rehabilitated fell on deaf ears when it was revealed that he had earlier received a bond for being armed with the intent to commit an indictable offence, the conditions of that bond being that he sought alcohol rehabilitation. Kennedy had failed to do this so the chances of rehabilitation were slim.

Victim impact statements were tendered to the court by Debara's mother Ann, father Roger and sister Josephine, detailing Debara's love of life, the plans she had for the future, and the tremendous hole her death had left in their lives. It was clear to the court, and to the sentencing judge, that Debara was much loved and would be greatly missed.

In summing up, Justice Bellew said:

> Exactly what it was that motivated the offender to act in the manner in which he did remains unexplained. Some of his actions were, as the Crown submitted, bizarre. What is clear however, is that although there is no evidence to suggest the offender's attack was pre-planned, it was nevertheless brutal and sustained. It involved a high degree of violence with repeated use of the fists and resulted in a multitude of injuries being inflicted upon the deceased. It follows that this was, on any view, an offence of significant objective seriousness.[98]

Justice Bellew then handed down his sentence. Adam John Kennedy was sentenced to 23 years and four months in jail, with a minimum of 17 years and six months; he will become eligible for parole in 2031.

Despite all the evidence to the contrary, the media still insisted on reporting on the crime as 'toy boy murders lover to stop her return to sex work'. The fact that this was a man clearly in a dangerous state of alcoholism, the fact that he was a controlling, abusive partner, and the fact that she threatened his sense of control by trying to end their relationship, escaped them. Those details were hardly as titillating as toy boys and sex for sale.

Debara's mother had the final say after sentencing. Overcome with grief and anger, she summed it up perfectly as Kennedy was led from the court, yelling at him, 'At least you get your life, Debbie doesn't. At least you can turn over in bed. Hope you're bloody satisfied.'[99]

A Dream Cut Short
MAYANG PRASETYO
4 October 2014

A mainstream Australian newspaper screamed the headline on their front page: 'Monster Chef and the Shemale', and to emphasise their point they placed a provocative image of a young Asian woman posing on a beach in a bikini. The writer practically salivated, stumbling to fit as many salacious details into their limited word count as would fit. She was a transgendered, high-class sex worker, and her husband had chopped her up and cooked her.

The reader might be forgiven for thinking that her sex work had something to do with her murder, that her poor husband had grown tired of all those men she had sex with, or become jealous. That she was Jezebel, and had somehow brought this misfortune on herself. Especially when the rest of the article revealed itself, when it became apparent that the man had run from police, hidden in an industrial-sized wheelie bin, and slashed his own throat. At the end of the article there was a prompt that if anyone was feeling suicidal, here was the Lifeline number. Was there also something about domestic violence? That if a woman felt she was at risk of harm from her partner there was also a number to ring? Either the journalist had reached their word limit, or it wasn't important to the story.

The real story was that a young man had killed his partner and then when his crime was discovered, committed suicide. However, it took a huge social media backlash and the gathering of tens of thousands of signatures before the Brisbane *Courier Mail* issued a quasi-apology.

In some ways the damage had already been done. The media showed contempt for a young woman who had been brutally murdered, by splashing near-naked photos of her across pages of newsprint and websites. It was disrespectful of the media to label her a high-class prostitute, even if that was how she earned her living. The 27-year-old woman was dead – murdered – and the media chose to victimise her all over again.

***

Teneriffe is an inner-city suburb of Brisbane. It lies two and a half kilometres north of the CBD, safely away from the hordes of tourists who descend on the city every day, and near enough for all the best of Brisbane to be at your fingertips. The former industrial area has undergone gentrification in recent years. It's trendy to live in Teneriffe, and the neighbourhood has attracted a young, cashed-up population and a large contingent of gay men and lesbians.

It was into this neighbourhood that Marcus Volke and his partner, Mayang Prasetyo, moved in 2014. They had married in Denmark on 1 August 2013. However, their relationship wasn't legally recognised in Australia, as Mayang was still – in the eyes of the law – a man.

Their apartment block was new, and Marcus and Mayang moved into unit 3 on the ground floor. Other residents didn't have time to get to know the young couple, as many of them were busy moving in and settling down themselves. There were reports of yelling and shouting, of fights coming from unit 3, but those stories would not be shared until later.

And then there was the smell.

One resident, Courtney Reichart, told the ABC she first noticed the smell in the foyer, and said it got worse every day. 'On Saturday when I came out for a walk, it made your eyes water, it made you want to be sick. It makes you feel sick that that poor girl sat there for however many days and we've been walking past, living our lives and thinking "what's that smell?" but you don't put two and two together … you don't think that a bad smell equals murder.'[100]

The beginning of the end came with a phone call from Marcus Volke to an electrician. It was Saturday morning, 4 October 2014, when Scottish-born Brad Coyne answered his phone.

'Yeah, I've got a bit of a problem. I was cooking on my stove. It's an electric stove and the stock boiled over, dripping down and, um, got in the oven.' The voice was young, male, knockabout Aussie. 'And it basically made this big bang and then all my power turned off. Does it sound like something you'd be able to fix today?'[101]

Brad Coyne arrived at the Teneriffe apartment block and even as he walked through the foyer he could smell something strange. It was stranger, more pungent when Marcus Volke opened the door to his ground floor apartment.

'You have to mind the smell,' Volke said, and he told the electrician he was a chef, and he had been cooking pig's broth.

In the kitchen Coyne saw an industrial-sized pot, a colander, bleach and rubber gloves. The whole time Coyne was in the apartment he felt uncomfortable.

On the way out Coyne had a word to someone from building

management and told them there was something going on in unit 3. Building management called the police.

When police knocked on Volke's door, he opened it. They noticed he had a knife in his hand. He obviously figured that the game was up and he ran through the apartment, went out through a sliding door and disappeared over his balcony. Volke sprinted down the street and around a corner. He was looking for somewhere to hide and he found it around another corner – an industrial-sized wheelie bin. Volk clambered in and closed the lid.

Meanwhile, police gave chase. They called for backup – including the canine unit – and cordoned off the area. It didn't take long to discover Volke's hiding place and, guns drawn, they surrounded him. He wouldn't come out, so police tipped the bin over. The lifeless body of 28-year-old Volke spilled out into the street. He had slashed his own throat.

When police and crime scene officers went back to the apartment, they were met with horrifying sights. Although they refused to confirm the electrician's story that it was Mayang's feet that Volke had been boiling on the stove, they also didn't deny it. They also wouldn't officially confirm the report that Mayang's head and arms were in plastic bags and stuffed in the couple's washing machine.

As the killer had already been discovered, there was little to investigate in the murder of Mayang Prasetyo. The secrets of what really happened behind the closed doors of their apartment were taken to the grave when Marcus Volke committed suicide. A neighbour told police he had seen Volke days earlier with cuts on his hands. When asked what happened, Volke said his girlfriend had come at him with a knife. She was crazy, he said, and they'd had a fight that got out of control. Another neighbour had heard shouting and screaming coming from the apartment earlier in the week. They didn't pay too much attention; it was none of their business. And then there was that smell, first noticed in the middle of the week, which had become eye-watering by Saturday. It was the stench of decomposition that lingered in the foyer.

***

Mayang Prasetyo was born in Bandar Lampung in the south of Sumatra, Indonesia. She was born a male and her mother named him Febri Andriansyah. Febri was raised with two younger sisters. In Lampung as he grew up, he owned and ran a pet shop. It was at the age of 22 that Febri told his mother that he wanted to become a woman. His mother, Nining Sukarno, always thought her son was more like a girl, and was completely supportive of Febri's wishes.

Febri became Mayang; she chose that name because she admired Indonesian singer Mayang Sari. Prasetyo was the name of an old boyfriend. Her first round of operations, the beginning of her metamorphosis, was in Thailand on 19 March 2009, where she underwent breast augmentation surgery.

Friends described Mayang as loud, spirited, elegant and insightful. She was gentle and kind, someone who drew people to her. She moved to Australia where she worked as a high-class transgender escort. She regularly sent money home to help her family out, and she paid to put her sisters through school.

Mayang worked in Melbourne at the Pleasure Dome. It was here that she met Marcus Volke who was also working in the sex industry at the time. After Mayang's murder, the owner of the Pleasure Dome gave an interview in which he claimed that he was aware Volke had previously assaulted Mayang. He also said it was Volke who convinced her to leave the escort agency and work privately.

Volke told his friends they met on a cruise ship where they were both working as chefs and travelling around the world. In 2013, the couple were living in Copenhagen, and both working in the sex industry. They moved to Teneriffe in 2014.

Marcus Volke was born and raised in Ballarat, Victoria. Friends and family were shocked to learn that his life had come to such a grisly end, and couldn't understand it. They described him as a gentle, animal-loving vegetarian who was careful with his nutrition and looked after his body. He didn't seem like the type of person who would harm anyone, let alone be responsible for such a gruesome, violent crime. Perhaps it's a timely reinforcement that there is no type.

As police investigated the end of Mayang Prasetyo's life, it was almost stranger than fiction. It didn't matter what labels the media attached to this exotic young woman. Being transgender didn't kill her, neither did sex work. It was the man she trusted and loved, and shared her life with.

The last time Nining Sukarno spoke to her daughter it was in a phone call not long before she died. Nining had the impression that Mayang was restless in Brisbane, that she was searching for something else. In the end, after the crime scene technicians had finished their work, and the coroner had tried to coax the story from Mayang, the Australian and Indonesian governments joined forces to repatriate Mayang's body.

Home to her mother. Home to Bandar Lampung. Where they laid her to rest.

TING FANG
1 January 2015

Ting Fang lived in Sydney. She was a 25-year-old Chinese national who came to Australia to work. She was employed by an escort agency and at the end of December 2014, Ting flew to Adelaide and booked herself into the Grand Chancellor Hotel in the city.

Hotel staff became aware of a problem when, on New Year's Day, they went to investigate reports that water had flooded into the corridor and into the room below. The discovery was gruesome. Ting Fang's jugular veins, both internal and external, had been cut. Police believe that a window cleaning blade was the murder weapon. It was days before a formal identification could be made, and relatives notified through the Department of Foreign Affairs.

Police have charged an Adelaide man with her murder, and the case will go to trial late in 2015.

TIFFANY TAYLOR
12 July 2015

Tiffany Taylor was just 16 years old and five months' pregnant when she disappeared. She was living with her boyfriend of four years, Greg Hill, at the Waterford West Hotel in Brisbane. Greg was unaware that his girlfriend was earning money by offering sex in exchange for money on an online dating website.

On 12 July 2015, Tiffany was seen getting into a car driven by a 60-year-old man. Police believe they drove 15 kilometres to an industrial estate at Larapinta, then a further 40 kilometres to the Brisbane Valley. In spite of an extensive search, Tiffany's body has not been recovered. Police have charged a man with her murder and the case will go to trial in 2016.

Not Forgotten

INDEX OF VICTIMS: MISSING AND MURDERED SINCE 1970

Since 1970 more than 65 Australian sex workers have been murdered, and 54 per cent of those murders remain unsolved. Compare this to the overall rate of homicide in Australia where only 11 per cent of all murders have not yet been solved, and more questions than answers are raised. In fairness, random crimes and crimes against a stranger are the most difficult to solve.[102]

We would love to have been able to write full stories about all these women, but if nothing else we hope that this list shows that they all matter to us. The following is not a complete list of all victims since 1970 – there are women who have disappeared that we know nothing about.

ACKNOWLEDGEMENTS

Writing *Invisible Women* has meant confronting issues, many of which are still considered taboo by society; for that reason many of the people we want to thank cannot be named. However, we want to say thank you to the women who have inspired, humbled and encouraged us to keep on writing in those moments when it all felt too hard. We can't let the moment pass without a shout-out to Sally Tonkin, CEO of St Kilda Gatehouse, for being generous with her time, and all the workers and volunteers.

Thank you to The Five Mile Press and Echo Publishing, especially our commissioning editor, Julia Taylor, for having faith in the idea that a book about murdered sex workers was a story worth telling. Our editor, Kyla Petrilli, deserves a medal for her patience and skill. Luke Causby, our cover designer, and Shaun Jury, our internal designer, have done an amazing job – thank you.

We're both proud to be part of Sisters in Crime, and couldn't be as brave or as energetic without their support and encouragement. Even closer to home we have a loose collection of friends who form the Bittern Writer's group. Coffee, hugs, cupcakes and laughter have helped fuel us on this long and challenging journey.

Finally, to our families, and those friends we love fiercely – you rock. And the pets, always the pets, thanks for the cuddles.

Notes

1 Figures from Scarlet Alliance, the national sex worker body, who collated the numbers from the state-based sex worker organisations. However, these figures are an estimate. By the nature of the work it is impossible to accurately assess figures.

2 Roxburgh, Amanda, Louisa Degenhardt and Jan Copeland, 'Posttraumatic stress disorder among female sex workers in the greater Sydney area, Australia', *BMC Psychiatry*, 2006; 6: 24.

3 Perkins, Roberta, 'The Working Lives of Prostitutes'. In: *Working Girls: Prostitutes, their Life and Social Control*, Australian Institute of Criminology, Canberra, May 1991.

4 'Green River Killer avoids death in plea deal', CNN.com, 6 November 2003.

5 Milman, Oliver, 'Adrian Bayley was on parole when he murdered Jill Meagher', *The Guardian* (Australia), 11 June 2013.

6 Sutton, Candice, 'Family ties in Valley', *The Sun-Herald*, 9 March 2003.

7 'In Tracy's Corner', *Australian Story*, ABC1, 12 May 2014.

8 'In Tracy's Corner', *Australian Story*, ABC1, 12 May 2014.

9 'In Tracy's Corner', *Australian Story*, ABC1, 12 May 2014.

10 Wills, Juliet, *Dirty Girls: The State Sanctioned Murder of Brothel Madam Shirley Finn* [Kindle Edition], Alto Books Pty Ltd, Australia, 9 December 2014.

11 Wills, Juliet, *Dirty Girls: The State Sanctioned Murder of Brother Madam Shirley Finn* [Kindle Edition], Alto Books Pty Ltd, Australia, 9 December 2014.

12 'Shirley Finn cold case: Former cop reveals new details about 1975 murder of brothel madam', *PerthNow Sunday Times*, 21 May 2015.

13 Cordell, Michael, 'Sallie-Anne: Why the Girl in the Fast Lane had to be Murdered', *Sydney Morning Herald*, 17 January 1987.

14 Smith, Arthur Stanley and Tom Noble, *Neddy: The Life and Crimes of Arthur Stanley Smith*, Kerr Publishing, Sydney, 31 December 1993.

15 Dale, John, *Huckstepp: A Dangerous Life*, Xoum Publishing, Australia, 1 May 2014.

16 Duffy, Michael, 'Pulling the trigger on corruption', *Sydney Morning Herald*, 20 November 2011.

17 Cordell, Michael, 'Sallie-Anne: Why the Girl in the Fast Lane had to be Murdered', *Sydney Morning Herald*, 17 January 1987.

18 Cordell, Michael, 'Sallie-Anne: Why the Girl in the Fast Lane had to be Murdered', *Sydney Morning Herald*, 17 January 1987.

19 Cordell, Michael, 'Sallie-Anne: Why the Girl in the Fast Lane had to be Murdered', *Sydney Morning Herald*, 17 January 1987.

20 Cordell, Michael, 'Sallie-Anne: Why the Girl in the Fast Lane had to be Murdered', *Sydney Morning Herald*, 17 January 1987.

21 Cordell, Michael, 'Sallie-Anne: Why the Girl in the Fast Lane had to be Murdered', *Sydney Morning Herald*, 17 January 1987.

22 Cordell, Michael, 'Sallie-Anne: Why the Girl in the Fast Lane had to be Murdered', *Sydney Morning Herald*, 17 January 1987.

23 Cordell, Michael, 'Sallie-Anne: Why the Girl in the Fast Lane had to be Murdered', *Sydney Morning Herald*, 17 January 1987.

24 Cordell, Michael, 'Sallie-Anne: Why the Girl in the Fast Lane had to be Murdered', *Sydney Morning Herald*, 17 January 1987.

25 Reilly, Tom, 'Richards accused of being a hard man in the past', *Sydney Morning Herald*, 9 December 2010.

26 Cordell, Michael, 'Sallie-Anne: Why the Girl in the Fast Lane had to be Murdered', *Sydney Morning Herald*, 17 January 1987.

27 Dale, John, *Huckstepp: A Dangerous Life*, Xoum Publishing, Australia, 1 May 2014.

28 Cordell, Michael, 'Sallie-Anne: Why the Girl in the Fast Lane had to be Murdered', *Sydney Morning Herald*, 17 January 1987.

29 Dale, John, *Huckstepp: A Dangerous Life*, Xoum Publishing, Australia, 1 May 2014.

30 Dale, John, *Huckstepp: A Dangerous Life*, Xoum Publishing, Australia, 1 May 2014.

31 Dale, John, *Huckstepp: A Dangerous Life*, Xoum Publishing, Australia, 1 May 2014.

32 Fife-Yeomans, Janet, *Killing Jodie*, Penguin Books, Australia, 2007.

33 R v Paterson (No 4) [2014] NSWSC 162 (3 March 2014).

34 R v Paterson (No 4) [2014] NSWSC 162 (3 March 2014).

35 R v Paterson (No 4) [2014] NSWSC 162 (3 March 2014).

36 Inquest – Revelle Balmain, NSW State Coroner's Court, Glebe, May 1999.

37 Anderson, Paul, '"Everyman" serial killer Bandali Debs pays price for murders of officers Gary Silk and Rodney Miller, sex workers Kristy Harty and Donna Hicks', *Herald Sun*, 28 May 2013.

38 Moor, Keith, 'Bandali Debs turned his gun on police officers, sex workers', *Herald Sun*, 12 December 2011.

39 R v Debs (2007) VSC 220 (22 June 2007).

40 R v Debs (2012) NSWSC 119 (24 February 2012).

41 Silvester, John, 'Grave secrets', *The Age*, 19 November 2005.

42 R v Dupas (No 2) [2005] VSCA 212 (26 August 2005).

43 R v Dupas (No 2) [2005] VSCA 212 (26 August 2005).

44 Queensland Police Media Release: 'Police continue to search for answers', 16 June 2003.

45 Queensland Police Media Release: 'Police continue to search for answers', 16 June 2003.

46 Aamodt, MG, 'Serial killer statistics', 6 September 2014. Retrieved 8 October 2015 from http://maamodt.asp.radford.edu/serial killer information center/project description.htm.

47 McFarlane, Duncan, 'Into the Valley', *The Australian*, 8 March 2003.

48 MacFarlane, Duncan, 'Drug need outweighs dread of lover's killer', *The Australian*, 3 March 2003.

49 Pavey, Ainsley, 'Daughter of murdered prostitute plans to stare down killer – How could he hurt my loving mother?', *Sunday Courier Mail*, 2 October 2005.

50 'NZ-born prostitute had dungeon in NZ, says friend', *The New Zealand Herald*, 3 March 2003.

51 Edmistone, Leanne, 'Anglers heard scream thought it was a loud bird', *The Courier Mail*, 16 May 2005.

52 'People get murdered here. That's the Valley', *The Age*, 8 March 2003.

53 'People get murdered here. That's the Valley', *The Age*, 8 March 2003.

54 Doneman, Paula, 'Killer of a catch', *The Courier Mail*, 29 April 2006.

55 Earl, Ed, 'Crimebusters Anonymous', *The Bulletin*, 24 May 2008.

56 'Two life terms for serial killer', Murderpedia, 12 April 2006. Retrieved 8 October 2015 from http://murderpedia.org.

57 'Two life terms for serial killer', Murderpedia, 12 April 2006. Retrieved 8 October 2015 from http://murderpedia.org.

58 'Who Was Kelly Hodge?', *The Age*, 6 September 2003.

59 The Queen v Novica Jakimov, Supreme Court of Victoria, Court of Appeal, 8 February 2007.

60 'Who Was Kelly Hodge?', *The Age*, 6 September 2003.

61 'Mother of murdered pregnant woman Sandra Cawthorne appeals to public for help', *The Daily Telegraph*, 15 April 2014.

62 Hart, Karen, 'A daughter's wayward path leads to a violent end', *The Age*, 22 July 2004.

63 Minchin, Liz and Jewel Topsfield, 'Streetwalkers lose in the blame game', *The Age*, 24 July 2004.

64 Minchin, Liz and Jewel Topsfield, 'Streetwalkers lose in the blame game', *The Age*, 24 July 2004.

65 R v Detenamo [2007] VSCA 160 (23 August 2007).

66 R v Detenamo [2007] VSCA 160 (23 August 2007).

67 R v Detenamo [2007] VSCA 160 (23 August 2007).

68 R v Detenamo [2005] VSC 411 (14 December 2005).

69 R v Detenamo [2005] VSC 411 (14 December 2005).

70 Oliver, Brian, *The Commonwealth Games: Extraordinary Stories behind the Medals*, A & C Black, London, 22 May 2014.

71 Findings of Inquest – Leanne Thompson, Office of the State Coroner, Brisbane Coroner's Court, Coroner John Lock, 3 May 2013.

72 Inquest into the death of Andrew Scott Anderson, Christine Clements, Deputy State Coroner Findings, Office of the State Coroner, 16 October 2009.

73 Findings of Inquest – Leanne Thompson, Coroner John Lock, Office of the State Coroner, Brisbane Coroner's Court, 3 May 2013.

74 Findings of Inquest – Leanne Thompson, Coroner John Lock, Office of the State Coroner, Brisbane Coroner's Court, 3 May 2013.

75 Findings of Inquest – Leanne Thompson, Coroner John Lock, Office of the State Coroner, Brisbane Coroner's Court, 3 May 2013.

76 Findings of Inquest – Leanne Thompson, Coroner John Lock, Office of the State Coroner, Brisbane Coroner's Court, 3 May 2013.

77 Callinan, Rory, 'O'Sachy pleaded guilty to strangling, stabbing assaults on former girlfriends', *The Australian*, 5 April 2011.

78 Callinan, Rory, 'O'Sachy pleaded guilty to strangling, stabbing assaults on former girlfriends', *The Australian*, 5 April 2011.

79 Callinan, Rory, 'O'Sachy pleaded guilty to strangling, stabbing assaults on former girlfriends', *The Australian*, 5 April 2011.

80 R v Malcolm POTTS [2010] NSWSC 731 (23 July 2010).

81 R v Malcolm POTTS [2010] NSWSC 731 (23 July 2010).

82 R v David John Dunn, Supreme Court of NSW, 26 March 2013.

83 'Prostitute axe killer jailed as judge tries to console family', *Sydney Morning Herald*, 27 March 2013.

84 'Prostitute axe killer jailed as judge tries to console family', *Sydney Morning Herald*, 27 March 2013.

85 Paradies, K, 'Murderer sentenced to life in jail for killing prostitute', *Central Telegraph*, 20 February 2013.

86 Anderson, Paul, 'Extreme stripper and murder victim Johanna "Jazzy O" Martin's incredible double life', *Herald Sun*, 2 July 2015.

87 Anderson, Paul, 'Extreme stripper and murder victim Johanna "Jazzy O" Martin's incredible double life', *Herald Sun*, 2 July 2015.

88 Anderson, Paul, 'Extreme stripper and murder victim Johanna "Jazzy O" Martin's incredible double life', *Herald Sun*, 2 July 2015.

89 McMahon, Neil, 'Mother, nanna, stripper: who was Jazzy O?', *The Age*, 6 November 2011.

90 Constantinou v The Queen [2015] VSCA 177 (2 July 2015).

91 Constantinou v The Queen [2015] VSCA 177 (2 July 2015).

92 Constantinou v The Queen [2015] VSCA 177 (2 July 2015).

93 Ensor, Blair and Seamus Boyer, '"Toy boy" accused of Kiwi's murder', *The Dominion Post*, 12 May 2012.

94 Ensor, Blair and Seamus Boyer, '"Toy boy" accused of Kiwi's murder', *The Dominion Post*, 12 May 2012.

95 R v Kennedy [2013] NSWSC 1940 (20 December 2013).

96 R v Kennedy [2013] NSWSC 1940 (20 December 2013).

97 R v Kennedy [2013] NSWSC 1940 (20 December 2013).

98 R v Kennedy [2013] NSWSC 1940 (20 December 2013).

99 'Drunken killer gets 17-year minimum', *Geelong Advertiser*, 20 December 2013.

100 Moncur, James, '"He was boiling her feet when I walked in": Electrician describes moment he saw killer cooking his wife', *The Mirror*, 10 October 2014.

101 Moncur, James, '"He was boiling her feet when I walked in": Electrician describes moment he saw killer cooking his wife', *The Mirror*, 10 October 2014.

102 Mouzos, Jenny and Damon Muller, 'Solvability Factors of Homicide in Australia: an exploratory analysis', Australian Institute of Criminology, October 2001.